CITIZENS' REFERENCE BOOK
VOLUME I

# CITIZENS' REFERENCE BOOK

## A TEXTBOOK FOR ADULT BEGINNERS
## IN TWO VOLUMES
### VOLUME I

By ELIZABETH C. MORRISS

*Director Community Schools*
*Buncombe County, North Carolina*

WITH AN INTRODUCTION

By HOWARD W. ODUM

*Director Institute for Research in Social Science*
*University of North Carolina*

CHAPEL HILL
THE UNIVERSITY OF NORTH CAROLINA PRESS
1936

*First Printing, February 1927*
*Second Printing, March 1928*
*Third Printing, February 1934*
*Fourth Printing, February 1935*
*Fifth Printing, March 1936*

COMPOSITION BY THE SEEMAN PRESS, DURHAM, NORTH CAROLINA

# Preface

*The Citizens' Reference Book* has been prepared primarily to meet the interests and needs of native adult beginners. It has, however, also been found useful with foreign-born adult elementary students. Much of the teaching in adult evening schools is done by day school teachers, who have insufficient time for detailed preparation of work for their classes. It is hoped that the lessons in this book may help in relieving this situation.

A large part of the material has been tried out in class work in adult schools and with individual pupils in their homes.

The central idea of the reading lessons is a happy, normal home, with high standards in health, proper food, thrift, education, recreation, coöperation, and citizenship, and the activities connecting the home with school, church, and community. This theme was chosen because the average age of the adult beginners is thirty years and most of them have a number of young children, in whose lives they are the strongest influence during their most impressionable years. The purpose of including a title for each reading lesson is two-fold: first, for the teacher's use in giving to the pupil the central thought of the lesson; second, for the pupil's use, a little later on in the course, in learning how to use a table of contents. A steady aim throughout the course is to implant a love of good reading. In connection with each reading lesson the development on board and in mimeographed sheets of new stories, using the same words together with those appearing in previous lessons, will serve to relate the material more closely to the experiences of the students and to give additional repetitions of the words in new relationships. The lessons were developed in connection with actual school and community plans and programs, and will be found to be most helpful if used in such relationships.

The Ayres list of three hundred words most used has been made the basis of the reading lessons, and each of the three hundred words has been included in the sixty-lesson course. (Forty of these reading lessons are found in Book One and the remaining twenty in Book Two of the *Citizens' Reference Book.*) All of the three hundred words of the Ayres list, with the exception of forty-three, are included in the first five hundred of Dr. Thorndike's word list. In sixty lessons the average pupil can probably learn the spelling of these three hundred words and approximately two hundred of the three hundred other words included in the sixty-lesson reading course.

The selected word groups have been chosen after much trying out in class and after consultation with the Directors of Adult

Education in South Carolina, Arkansas, and Massachusetts. These groups are included for purposes of ready reference. The words, and also the group headings, are arranged alphabetically. If pupils become familiar with the group headings and can find them quickly, they can soon find the correct spelling of almost any word they need in their letter writing. Drill in finding the different headings will prove helpful and interesting. Drill in reading the words under each heading will soon enable pupils to turn quickly to the words they need.

An interesting fact, that is more helpful than would be at first imagined, is that the sequence of the alphabet is known to practically every adult beginner. They do not know the letters by sight, either in print or script, but they can say them. For this reason, the alphabet—both small and capital letters and both in print and in script—is put at the beginning of the word list. By beginning with "A" and coming down the list, the pupil can find any letter asked for. When this has been done a great many times, he begins to recognize the forms of the letters. Changing print to script is accomplished by the same device after the printed letters are learned.

The lessons in phonics have been worked out in great detail and tried out successfully with native adult beginners. Phonics can be of great value to the adult beginner, particularly in the recognition of new words, if the approach to the subject can be made naturally and with no self consciousness on his part. After he once puzzles out a new word for himself, he is an enthusiastic convert. This section should be used by the teacher along with the first twenty-lesson course in reading. Careful use and adaptation of this material by the teacher can be of great help from the beginning. This section is placed in the back of the book, not because it is unimportant, but because it can be used only under the direction of the teacher.

Because the dictionary habit is of first importance in self-education, much care has been given to making the use of the dictionary a simple and an easy matter. Experience has shown that unless much drill is given in the use of alphabetical word lists and in lessons preparatory to the use of the dictionary very little use is made of it, because of the many unfamiliar obstacles to be overcome in the process.

The goal, which it is hoped the pupils may reach through the writing lessons, is legibility, with attention given to correct height, spacing, and slant.

Certain very definite aims have been kept clearly in mind in developing the twenty lessons in English: (1) the ability to speak more freely, correctly, and interestingly; (2) the ability to give three or four correct sentences on one subject; (3) the correct use of capitals and most commonly used punctuation marks; (4) the ability to copy and to take from dictation simple sentences, with ease and without error; (5) the ability to write correctly very simple personal and business letters. The underlying thought that decided the details of these lessons is that "Only *correct* practice makes perfect."

The lessons in arithmetic have been developed with the underlying purpose of enabling the adult pupil to formulate the problems that come up in his every day life and to solve them with accuracy and intelligence.

That this book may be of real value in raising the standards of citizenship and of parenthood in the group of adult beginners, who "missed their chanst," and that it may contribute to the growth and happiness of individual lives is our sincere desire.

Surely reading, writing, and arithmetic, the elements of the mother tongue, a fair knowledge of our country's history and government and of the fundamentals of a happy, normal home environment are the birthright of every American.

In making this book, generous assistance was received from men and women expert in the different subjects undertaken. Heartiest thanks are due:

In counsel and advice—Dr. Edward L. Thorndike, Mr. L. R. Alderman, Dr. Howard W. Odum, Mr. F. P. Keppel, Mr. Morse A. Cartwright, Mr. Robert C. Deming, Miss Wil Lou Gray, Miss Willie Lawson, Miss Mary L. Guyton, Miss Marguerite Burnett, and Mr. John W. Lewis.

In testing material in class work with adult beginners and in many practical suggestions—Misses Eva Edgerton, Maud Worley, H. Ethel Ray, Jennie L. Whitaker, and Mrs. J. M. Day.

In reading—Miss Ila Johnston, Miss Blanche E. Shaffer (in Home Economics material), Mrs. Sheldon Leavitt, and the National Child Welfare Association.

In writing—Mrs. L. M. Hodges and Mr. A. J. Lyman.

In word lists—Dr. Alfred Ayres, Dr. Edward L. Thorndike, Dr. Franklin K. Jones, Miss Wil Lou Gray, Miss Willie Lawson, and Mr. Charles M. Herlihy.

In arithmetic—Mrs. Rose Goodwin.

In illustrations—Especial thanks are due Miss Margaret Harper who has generously devoted much time to preparing special drawings for the two volumes. Her work has been kindly supplemented by The National Child Welfare Association, Metropolitan Life Insurance Company, Indiana Tuberculosis Association, and Delaware Parent-Teacher Association.

ELIZABETH C. MORRISS.

ASHEVILLE, N. C.,
*January, 1927.*

# Introduction

*The Citizens' Reference Book* is a valuable contribution to the modern functional curriculum and will be welcomed alike by educators, social workers, and students of society. These volumes have grown directly out of first hand experience and from the actual needs of older citizens in community schools. The importance of this fact was recognized by Professor E. L. Thorndike, of Columbia University, who referred to *The Citizens' Reference Book* as "a good piece of work by a person with experience in the field, who has given much time and thought to the matter."

The story of the Buncombe County community schools, in which Mrs. Morriss, with the cordial coöperation of the county superintendent of schools, the county superintendent of public welfare, and the citizens and agencies of Asheville, has developed her teaching method, is one of the most interesting in the annals of the American adult education movement. The program and efforts which have formed the background upon which these texts were built reflect a number of fundamental features. Beginning in a small way with voluntary leadership and teaching, they have grown into consolidated evening schools as a regular part of the county system of education, utilizing buildings, school trucks, and other facilities. Step by step and grade by grade, methods and content have been evolved together, so that theory and practice are merged in a natural product, effective both for teaching and community organization.

The content, methods, and spirit of *The Citizens' Reference Book* and the actual school work upon which it was built have emphasized in peculiarly effective ways the social objectives of education. In organizing her lessons around fundamental interests and community efforts, Mrs. Morriss has planned wisely not only for this generation, but for starting well the children of her adult learners into future paths of education and citizenship. Education, health, diet, work, play, thrift, and coöperation form a theoretical background, socially sound, easily translated into practical work. To these are added certain ethical concepts, which are entirely in accord with the most advanced principles of the modern educational theory and practice which look to the study and development of character, personality, and moral education. These interests and principles in turn are well presented in an admirable variety of selections representing language, literature, history, citizenship, and social emphasis.

Once again, *The Citizens' Reference Book* conforms to the newer and larger programs of adult education being developed in this country and abroad. One of the most significant of modern movements is this whole effort of adult education to develop continuity of learning and contacts, and to bridge the distance between the technician, education, government, and society on the one hand, and the popular constituency on the other. From its elementary stages in beginning education for adults through its various steps, including the continuation education of the alumni of our colleges and universities, the whole movement constitutes an epochal adventure in modern functional education. The movement in America was crystallized in the spring of 1926 by the organization of the American Association for Adult Education, which in turn is constantly in touch with the World Association for Adult Education. A number of important contributions have been made during the last year or two to this field. The most important are the volumes giving the result of the Carnegie Corporation studies. These include Peffer's *New School for Older Students,* Evans' *Educational Opportunities for Young Workers,* Noffsinger's *Correspondence Schools, Lyceums, and Chautauquas,* Hall-Quest's *The University Afield,* and the American Library Association volumes on libraries and adult education. Other important volumes are Keppel's *Education for Adults,* Joseph K. Hart's *Light from the North, Adult Education,* and Lindeman's *The Meaning of Adult Education.* These are samples of a rapidly growing literature, a full account of which is being prepared by Morse A. Cartwright, secretary of the American Association for Adult Education.

Mrs. Morriss may find cause for gratification that *The Citizens' Reference Book* not only does well its own specific task, but also becomes an admirable unit in the larger program and processes of adult education in the United States. It is offered in the University of North Carolina Social Study Series in the belief that it will meet an important need, not only in the South but throughout the United States.

HOWARD W. ODUM.

CHAPEL HILL,
*February 1, 1927.*

# Contents

PAGE

PREFACE . . . . . . . . . . . . . . . . v

INTRODUCTION . . . . . . . . . . . . . ix

READING: FIRST TWENTY-LESSON COURSE . . . 1

I. My Home. II. Work and Play. III. Home Work
and Home Play. IV. My Family. V. My School.
VI. School Tools. VII. Reading and Writing. VIII.
Day and Night Plans. IX. My Church. X. My
Friends. XI. My Children. XII. The Pleasures of
Reading. XIII. My Car. XIV. Plans for the Chil-
dren. XV. Education. XVI. Health. XVII. School
Party Plans. XVIII. What To Do. XIX. A School
Lunch Poster. XX. The Night School Party.

READING: SECOND TWENTY-LESSON COURSE . . 25

I. Who are You? II. More About You. III. A Bank
Account. IV. A Budget. V. Owning a Home. VI.
The Baby's Health. VII. The Baby's Bath. VIII.
Health Plans. IX. Balanced Meals. X. Balanced
Meals. XI. A Good School Lunch. XII. On Doing
Good. XIII. Good Citizenship. XIV. Good Citizen-
ship. XV. Advantages of a Consolidated School.
XVI. A Community Center. XVII. Community Party
Plans. XVIII. An Invitation. XIX. Joyful Progress.
XX. A Picnic.

ALPHABET (In Print and Script) . . . . . . 50

WORD LISTS . . . . . . . . . . . . . 51

1. Words used in each of the forty reading lessons.
2. Ayres List: 300 Words Most Used.
3. Thorndike List: First 500 Words.

TWENTY LESSONS PREPARATORY TO USE OF
    DICTIONARY . . . . . . . . . . . 61

PAGE

WRITING   .   .   .   .   .   .   .   .   .   .   .   .   .   69
First Twenty-Lesson Course.
Second Twenty-Lesson Course.

ENGLISH   .   .   .   .   .   .   .   .   .   .   .   .   .   89
First Twenty-Lesson Course.
Second Twenty-Lesson Course.

ARITHMETIC   .   .   .   .   .   .   .   .   .   .   .   .   109
First Twenty Lessons.
Second Twenty Lessons

PHONICS   .   .   .   .   .   .   .   .   .   .   .   .   .   149
Twenty Lessons for Use with First Twenty-
Lesson Course in Reading.

# CITIZENS' REFERENCE BOOK
## VOLUME I

# Reading
## First Twenty-Lesson Course

### Lesson I
### My Home

this   is   my   home   I   love

My home.
This is my home.
I love my home.

*I love my home!*

### Lesson II
### Work and Play

work   play   and   like   to   in

I work.
I play.
I work and I play.
I like to work.
I like to play.

[ 1 ]

I like to work in my home.
I like to play in my home.

*I like to play in my home.*

### Lesson III
### Home Work and Home Play

have    you    a    your    do

Have you a home?
Do you love your home?
Do you work and play in your home?
Do you like to work and to play in your home?
I have a home.
I love my home.
I like to work and to play in my home.

*I like to work and to play in my home.*

## Lesson IV
## My Family

mother   father   brother   sister   me

I love my mother and my father.
I love my sister and my brother.
My mother and my father love me.
My brother and my sister love me.
Have you a sister?

I have a sister.
Have you a brother?
I have a brother.
My brother likes to work.
My sister likes to play.
My mother and my father like my home.

*My mother and my father like my home.*

## Lesson V
### My School

go    school    read    write    note

I go to school.
Do you go to school?
I like to go to school.
I read in school.
I write in school.
I like to read.
I like to write.
I like to write in my notebook.
I like to read and to write in school.

I like to read and to write in my home.

Do you like to read and to write?

*Do you like to read and to write?*

## Lesson VI
## School Tools

book     own     from     with     what
        pencil    follow    up

I have a book.

I have my own book.

I read from my book.

Have you your own book?

Do you read from your own book?

I write in a book.

With what do you write?

I write with a pencil.

I write in my own book.

I write with my own pencil.

Do you write with your own pencil?

Do you write in your own book?

I write in my own book with my own pencil.

I like to have my own book and my own pencil.

I like to write in my own book with my own pencil.

### Follow Up Work

Write in your notebook:

*I like to write.*

## Lesson VII
### Reading and Writing

can name letter friends not soon

Can you read?

I can read in my book.

Can you write your name?

I can write my name.

Can you write a letter?

I can not write a letter.

I can soon write a letter to my friends.

I like to read to my mother.

I like to write my name in my book.

My brother can write a letter.

My mother and my father will write a letter to me.

### Follow Up Work

Write in your notebook:

*My mother will write to me.*

### Lesson VIII
### Day and Night Plans

the    day    night    sleep    at    stay

I work in the day.

I play in the day.

I go to the night school.

I sleep at night.

I do not stay late at the night school.

I do not work late at night.

My sister likes to sleep late in the day.

My father and my mother go to night school.

Can you write "day" and "night"?

I can write "day" and "night."

### Follow Up Work

Write in your notebook:

*I can soon write "today."*

### Lesson IX
### My Church

every on Sunday church them far

I do not work every day.

I do not work on Sunday.

I do not go to school on Sunday.

I go to church on Sunday.

I like to go to church on Sunday.

The church is not far from my home.

My mother and father like to go to church.

Do your sister and brother like to go to church?

My sister and brother like to go to church every Sunday.

I go to church with them.

I like to go to church with them.

**Follow Up Work**

Write in your notebook:

*I like to go to church!*

## Lesson X
## My Friends

see   some   kind   are   of   yes   am

I see my friends at church.

I see my friends at night school.

I like to go to see my friends.

I like to see my friends in my home.

Some of my friends work with me.

I am kind to my friends.

Do you like to work with your friends?

Are your friends kind to you?

Yes, my friends are kind to me.

I like to work with them.

My sister likes some of my friends.

My brother likes some of your friends.

My mother and my father are kind to my friends.

Some of my friends are in my home every day.

**Follow Up Work**

Write in your notebook:

*I like to see my friends in my home!*

### Lesson XI
### My Children

wife    son    daughter    baby    little
our    also

My wife and I have a son.

My wife and I have a daughter.

My wife and I have a little baby.

Our son and daughter like to go to school.

Our baby likes play.

My wife likes to play with the baby.

I like to play with the baby, also.

Our friends like our son.

Our friends like our daughter.

Our son and daughter like our home.

Follow Up Work

Write in your notebook:

*I like to play with the baby.*

### Lesson XII
### The Pleasures of Reading

husband    for    him    newspaper
Bible    good    sent

My husband reads to me.
I like for him to read to me.
He likes to read the newspaper.
He likes to read the Bible.
He likes to read good books.
My son reads at home.
My daughter reads good books
at school.
My friend sent a newspaper to
me.
I read the newspaper to my
mother.

My father reads the Bible at church on Sunday.

He reads the Bible at home every day.

**Follow Up Work**

Write in your notebook:

*I like to read good books!*

## Lesson XIII
### My Car

he     has     car     but     goes     his
takes     trips

I have a car.

I go to work in my car.

My father goes with me.

He has a car of his own.

But he likes to go to work with me.

He takes my mother to church
in his car.

I take my sister to school in my
car.

I take my brother and my mother
home in my car.

My baby sister likes to play in
the car.

My friends go on trips with me
in my car.

### Follow Up Work

Write in your notebook:

*I go to work in my car.*

### Lesson XIV
### Plans for the Children

be    want    healthy    citizens    make
we    been

My wife and I have been to night
school.

We want our children to go to
school.

We want our children to learn to read and write.

We want our children to play.

We want our children to work.

We want them to sleep at night.

We want them to go to church.

We want them to be healthy.

We want our children to be good children.

**Follow Up Work**

Write in your notebook:

*Our children will be good citizens!*

### Lesson XV
### Education

must   learn   cook   sew   come   shall

We must have a good school.

My wife and I want a good school for our children.

Our children will go to school every day.

They will learn to read and write.

They will learn to cook.

They will learn to sew.

They will learn to be good citizens.

We shall work for a good school.

My wife and I go to night school.

Our friends will come to night school.

Write in your notebook:

*We shall work for a good school.*

## Lesson XVI
## Health

rules     will     try     keep     well
food  eat

My wife and I love our children.
We want them to be healthy.
They learn health rules at school.
We learn health rules at night school.
We shall try to keep well.
We shall work in the day.
We shall play in the day.
We shall sleep at night.
My wife will cook good food.
We shall eat good food.

Write in your notebook:

*We shall try to keep well.*

## Lesson XVII
## School Party Plans

party    please    everybody    again
ask   us   something

We shall have a night school party.

We shall write a letter to our friends.

We shall ask our friends to come to our party.

We shall read and write for them.

We shall sing for them.

They will sing for us.

Everybody will have something to eat.

We shall try to please everybody.

We want our friends to come again.

We shall ask them to come again.

### Follow Up Work

Write a letter to a friend.

In this letter, ask him to come to our party.

## Lesson XVIII
### What to Do

find      that      begins      picture
paste      word

Find a word that begins with "a."

Write the word in your note-book.

Find a word that begins with "b."

Write the word in your note-book.

Find a picture of a book.

Paste the picture of the book in your notebook.

Find a word that begins with "c."

Write the word in your note-book.

Find a picture of a car.

Paste the picture in your note-book.

### Follow Up Work

Read the lesson to a friend.

## Lesson XIX
## A School Lunch Poster

made    poster    lunch    milk    bread
fruit    cut out

Make a good-cooking poster for our party.

Make a poster of a good school lunch.

Find a picture of milk.

Find a picture of bread.

Find a picture of some fruit.

Cut out the pictures.

Paste the pictures on the poster.

You have made a poster of a good school lunch for our friends to see.

Your poster will please our friends.

### Follow Up Work

Write in your notebook:

milk,    bread,    fruit,    lunch.

## Lesson XX
## The Night School Party

Teacher's Note: Several of the new words in this lesson have been learned in letter writing lessons.

end  term  show  prepare  business
gentlemen  sir  truly  or

This is the end of our school term.

We are having our night school party.

We shall show our friends what we have learned at night school.

We have learned to write our names.

We have learned to write letters to our friends.

We have learned to read.

We can read the Bible.

We can read the newspapers.

We can read letters from our fathers, our mothers, and our children.

We have learned to prepare food well.

We have learned to prepare school lunches for our children.

We have made a poster of a good school lunch.

We have learned the health rules.

We work and play in our homes.

Our friends come to see us in our homes.

We go to see our friends.

We want to be good citizens.

Our children will be good citizens.

### Follow Up Work

Write in your notebook:

"Gentlemen," "Sir," "truly."

Write a business letter.

Begin the letter with "Gentlemen" or "Dear Sir."

End the letter with "Yours truly."

# Reading
# Second Twenty-Lesson Course

### Lesson I
### Who Are You?

1. My name is.....................
2. This date is.....................
3. I live in...................County.
4. My address is....................
5. I was born in....................
(City, County, State)
6. I was in day school............years.
7. I work at.......................
(Place of employment)
8. I am.........married.
9. My wife's name is.................
10. My husband's name is.............
11. I have............children.
(number)
12. The names of my children are:.......,
    ..............., and ...........
13. I am.............years old.
14. I am in......grade in the night school.

**Follow Up Work**

Write these sentences in your notebook.
Write the names of three streets.

## Lesson II
### More About You

1. My house number is..............
2. My telephone number is...........
3. I can read...................books.
4. I can play......................
5. My church is....................
6. My lodge is.....................
7. My club is......................
8. My occupation is.................
9. My recreation is................
10. Our day school is...............
    (Name of school)
11. Our night school is..............
    (Name of school)
12. My friends,........., ..........,
    and......., need night school work.

**Follow Up Work**

Write these sentences in your notebook.

### Lesson III
## A Bank Account

I work every day but Sunday.

I receive money for my work.

I receive money at the end of each week.

My wife and I save some money each week for food.

We save some money for books.

We save some money for church on Sunday.

We save some money for our home.

We have a bank account.

We save money for this account each week.

Money in the bank works for us.

Our children will save for a bank account.

We like to save money each week for our home.

We expect to own our home.

### Follow Up Work

Write in your notebook how much money you save each week.

Write in your notebook how much money you save each month.

Courtesy of the Metropolitan Life Insurance Company.

## Lesson IV
## A Budget

Mr. White and his wife have a budget.
They want to own a home.
They use some money for rent.
They use some money for food.
They use some money for clothes.
They use some money for health.
They use some money for church.
They use some money for books.
They use some money for recreation.
They have a bank account, too.
They save money each week for a home.
The children save money for the bank account, too.
They save every cent they can.
Mr. White takes the money to the bank every Saturday for the savings account.
They will soon own a home.

### Follow Up Work

Find a picture of a home that you like.
Paste this picture in your notebook.
Write the words "My Home" under the picture.

Write in your notebook how much money you can save each week for a home like this.

Teacher's Note: Read to class, "Home, Sweet Home."

### Lesson V
## Owning a Home

Teacher's Note: This lesson may be omitted.

Mr. and Mrs. White will buy a lot with the money that they have saved.

They will find a book with plans for good houses.

They can not build a good house without a plan.

They will find a plan that they like.

They will find how much money they need for this plan.

They will use this plan for building the new house.

They want to own their home.

They will ask their friends to come to see them.

Their friends will be pleased to come.

The children will ask their friends to come to a party in the new home.

Everybody will see how a budget and a bank account can build a home.

### Follow Up Work

Find a book with good house plans in it.

Write a letter to a friend asking her to

come to a party.   End the letter, "Cordially yours."

Teacher's Note: Good plans make pretty houses.  No plans make ugly houses.

## Lesson VI
### The Baby's Health

Do you want your baby to be healthy? Then you will have to see that your baby has:

1. Regular habits.
2. Good food and drink.
3. Fresh air.
4. Rest and sleep.
5. Clean food and clothing.
6. Mother love.

### Follow Up Work

Find the name of a book that shows you how to keep your baby well.

Write a letter asking for this book.

Mail the letter.

Teacher's Note: The teacher should find out and have available information concerning city, county, state and national organizations from which information on the care of babies may be secured free or for a very small charge.  Some of these bulletins and pamphlets such as *Infant Care* issued by the Children's Bureau of the Department of Labor, Washington, D. C., would certainly be of interest to mothers.

## Lesson VII
### The Baby's Bath

Three nights a week, I fill the tub,*
And gaily baby takes a scrub,
It makes him clean and keeps him well,
It makes him happy as you can tell.

#### Follow Up Work

Make a poster: "Good Habits for a Baby."

Make another poster: "Good Habits for a Child."

Read yesterday's lesson.

* Text adapted from National Child Welfare Association poster and used by their courtesy.

Then see if you can say what a baby needs to keep him healthy.

## Lesson VIII
## Health Plans

Our children are going to school next month.

We want them to be healthy when they go.

The teacher told us to take them to the doctor.

Their eyes, teeth, and tonsils needed attention.

The doctor told us what to do.

We shall do what he told us for we want to make them healthy.

Fresh air, good food, clean clothes, rest, sleep, and play will keep them healthy.

They will do well in school.

The teacher will be pleased for they will soon learn to read and write.

### Follow Up Work

Write in your notebook two reasons why healthy children do well in school.

## Lesson IX
## Balanced Meals

My wife is a good cook.

She cooks for my children and me.

She cooks vegetables, eggs, cereals, and meat.

We like our children to eat vegetables, eggs, fruit, cereals, bread, butter and meat.

We like them to drink milk.

My wife keeps fruit in the house for the children.

They like fruit very much and they need it.

My wife gives the children fruit for their lunch.

My friend is not married.

He does not have such good food.

**Follow Up Work**

Name three vegetables.

Name three fruits.

Name three cereals.

Name three kinds of bread.

Write the names of the kinds of vegetables, fruits, cereals and breads in your notebook.

## Lesson X
## Balanced Meals
## A Good Breakfast—A Good Start

A Good Breakfast *

Milk                    Cereal

Egg                     Fruit

Bread and Butter

* Illustration copyright by the National Child Welfare Association and used through their courtesy.

Begin the day right.

Balance your meals.

Eat something from each group.

Cereals—breakfast foods.

Fats—butter, fat meat.

Vegetables and fruits—some of these every day.

Protein foods—meats, eggs.

Let milk be the balance wheel.

### Follow Up Work

Write in your notebook the names of the five food groups.

Write the name of one food in each group.

Paste a picture of the food after its name.

### Lesson XI
### A Good School Lunch

To-day is Thursday.

Mary is going to school.

I must give her some lunch.

I shall cut some bread quite thin.

I shall put some cheese on this bread.

She will like a tomato.

I shall put in a red apple, too.

I shall give her a bottle of milk.

I shall wrap these and put them in a lunch box.

Mary will have a good lunch.

**Follow Up Work**

Write in your notebook what you like to have in your lunch.

### Lesson XII
### On Doing Good

Do all the good you can
By all the means you can
In all the ways you can
In all the places you can
At all the times you can
To all the people you can
As long as ever you can.
—JOHN WESLEY.

**Follow Up Work**

Write in your notebook about a friend who does all the good he can to all the people he can.

### Lesson XIII
### Good Citizenship

The men and women in the schools for adults want to be good citizens.

They want their children to be good citizens.

They will learn the things a good citizen should know and do.

They will learn that:

A good citizen should know how to write his own letters.

A good citizen should know how to read the newspapers and the Bible.

A good citizen should know how to keep his own accounts.

A good citizen should have good food for his children.

A good citizen should keep his children well.

A good citizen should keep his children in school.

A good citizen should save money.

A good citizen should have a bank account.

A good citizen hopes to own his home.

A good citizen should work and play.

A good citizen should help his community.

Each school for adults will have a community project each month.

The men and women will plan some project that will help their community.

They will work on this project every week.

### Follow Up Work

Tell the school of some project that will help your community.

Ask all the men and women in the school to work on this project.

### Lesson XIV
### Good Citizenship

Mr. and Mrs. White are good citizens. They know that:

A good citizen should vote.

He should learn what is right.

Then he should vote for what he has learned is right.

He should pay his debts.

He should learn self-control.

He should be willing to pay his taxes.

He should have clean, wholesome thoughts.

Any man feels himself more of a man when he does these things.

### Follow Up Work

Ask the teacher to read to the school other things that a good citizen should do.

Write in your notebook about a man who is a good citizen of your community.

Write a letter to a woman, who is a good citizen of your community.

Begin the letter, "Dear Madam."

End the letter, "Respectfully yours."

In the letter, ask her to come to your school.

For the teacher to read to the class:
Characteristics of a good citizen.
Pledge of Allegiance.
How to salute the flag.

### Lesson XV

## Advantages of a Consolidated School

Mary and her brother are glad that they will soon be going to a consolidated school.

Their mother and father have worked for this school.

They knew that all the children needed a better school building.

They felt obliged to work for it.

Their children will have better teachers in the consolidated school.

The school will have better equipment.

The school term will be longer.

The school will be a wholesome and attractive community center.

The men and women will come to this community center for education and recreation.

They will be glad to pay taxes for building this consolidated school.

### Follow Up Work

Write in your notebook nine good things that a school of this kind will mean to your community.

### Lesson XVI
### A Community Center

We want our school to be a community center.

We shall have a party in our new consolidated school on Friday, the sixteenth.

All the men and women of the community will be invited to come.

We shall ask them to come at eight o'clock.

The children will come, too.

We shall have good music.

Some of the men will tell jokes.

Some of the women will tell stories.

Our teacher will read us a story from the Bible.

Everybody will play games.

Then, everybody will sing.

The good-cooking group will prepare refreshments.

The men and women will see the work of the day school children.

Everybody will be glad to see the work of the night school men and women.

This party will be our Community School project.

We want our party to be attractive to everybody in the community.

We must begin to make plans for our party, for we want everybody to have a good time.

### Follow Up Work

Write in your notebook the names of six games to be played at the party.

Write the names of six songs to be sung at the party.

### Lesson XVII
### Community Party Plans

When shall we have our school party?

At what time shall we ask our friends to come?

Where can we get cars for them?

Who will write the invitations?

Who will copy the programs?

What shall we have for refreshments?

What part of the refreshments will the women prepare?

What part of the refreshments will the girls prepare?

For what part of the refreshments will the men pay?

Who will make posters for the party?

Who will have charge of the games?

Who will have charge of the music?

Who will decorate the room?

Who will welcome our friends?

Who will put things in order after the party?

### Follow Up Work

Write in your notebook the names of the men and women who will be in charge of each of these things.

### Lesson XVIII
### An Invitation

Asheville, N. C.,
May 20, 1934.

Dear Friend:

The community school will have a party for everybody in our community on Thursday, May 24, 1934, at 7:30 p. m. in the new consolidated school building. We want you to be sure to come. We believe you will have a good time for we have prepared an attractive program.

Sincerely yours,

Mary White.

### Follow Up Work

Write an invitation to a friend, asking him to come to a party in your own school.

Ask him to write an answer to your invitation or to call you on the telephone.

## Lesson XIX
## Joyful Progress

A man learned to copy his name.

He had not learned the names of the letters, but he could copy them.

He was very proud of this.

He rushed to his friend with the copy of his name.

He said: "There she is, Bud! There's my name! I can't read her yet, but I can write her!"

### Follow Up Work

Write in your notebook some of the things you have learned since you came to night school.

## Lesson XX
## A Picnic

Mr. and Mrs. White are planning to have a picnic tomorrow for their own friends and for their children's friends.

If it doesn't rain, they will have it by the lake.

Everybody will take a good lunch.

Some of the people will row and some will swim.

Everybody will play games.

Everybody will sing.

If it should rain, they will have a party in their home.

Then they will play games, sing, and tell jokes and stories.

Mr. and Mrs. White believe that wholesome recreation will mean much to the people of their community.

Then, too, they like to have a good time.

### Follow Up Work

Read this to your children or to your friends:

"To be healthy and happy, we must all work, but we should play too."

"All work and no play makes Jack a dull boy."

Write in your notebook what you like to have in a picnic lunch.

Write in your notebook what games you like to have at a picnic.

# The Alphabet

| | | | | | | |
|---|---|---|---|---|---|---|
| A | a | *Aa* | | N | n | *Nn* |
| B | b | *Bb* | | O | o | *Oo* |
| C | c | *Cc* | | P | p | *Pp* |
| D | d | *Dd* | | Q | q | *Qq* |
| E | e | *Ee* | | R | r | *Rr* |
| F | f | *Ff* | | S | s | *Ss* |
| G | g | *Gg* | | T | t | *Tt* |
| H | h | *Hh* | | U | u | *Uu* |
| I | i | *Ii* | | V | v | *Vv* |
| J | j | *Jj* | | W | w | *Ww* |
| K | k | *Kk* | | X | x | *Xx* |
| L | l | *Ll* | | Y | y | *Yy* |
| M | m | *Mm* | | Z | z | *Zz* |

# Word Lists

For First Twenty-Lesson Course
in Reading

**1**
this
is
my
home
I
love

**2**
work
play
and
like
to
in

**3**
have
you
a
your
do

**4**
mother
father
brother
sister
me

**5**
go
to
school
read
write
note

**6**
book
own
from
pencil
with
what
follow
up

**7**
can
name
letter
friends
not
soon

**8**
the
day

night
sleep
at
stay

**9**
every
on
Sunday
church
them
far

**10**
see
some
kind
are
of
yes
am

**11**
wife
son
daughter
baby
little
our
also

**12**
husband
for
him
newspaper
Bible
good
sent

**13**
he
has
car
but
goes
his
takes
trips

**14**
be
want
healthy
citizens
make
we
been

[ 51 ]

**15**
must
learn
cook
sew
come
shall

**16**
rules
will
try
keep

well
food
eat

**17**
party
please
everybody
again
ask
us
something

**18**
find
that
begins
picture
paste
word

**19**
made
poster
lunch
milk
bread

fruit
cut out

**20**
end
term
show
prepare
business
gentleman
sir
truly
or

## For Second Twenty-Lesson Course in Reading

**1**
who
date
live
county
address
was
born
married
years
old
streets

**2**
more
about
house
telephone

lodge
club
occupation
recreation
need
sentences

**3**
receive
money
week
save
bank
account
each
they
how
expect

**4**
Mr.
White
budget
use
rent
clothes
cent
too
Saturday

**5**
Mrs.
buy
lot
plans
cordially
building

cannot
without

**6**
regular
then
habits
drink
fresh
air
rest
clean
mail

**7**
three
fill
tub

gaily
scrub
happy
tell
as
another
say
yesterday

**8**

their
next
when
teacher
doctor
eyes
teeth
tonsils
attention

**9**

vegetables
cereals
eggs
meat
butter
very
much
such
need

**10**

start
right
balance
meals
group

protein
wheel
five
after

**11**

put
cheese
tomato
red
apple
bottle
wrap
box
quite

**12**

by
means
ways
places
times
people
long
ever
all

**13**

men
women
adults
should
know
community
project
month

**14**

vote
**pay**
**taxes**
self
control
wholesome
thought
debts
feels

**15**

glad
consolidated
knew
better
equipment
attractive
center
education
obliged
nine

**16**

invited
music
jokes
stories
games
sing
refreshments
Friday
sixteenth
eight
o'clock

**17**

copy
programs
charge
decorate
room
welcome
after
where
girls

**18**

May
dear
sure
believe
sincerely
an
invitation
answer
call
Thursday

**19**

could
proud
rushed
said
there
she
can't
yet
her
things
since

| 20 | rain | swim | boy |
| picnic | lake | no | tomorrow |
| if | row | dull | time |
| doesn't | | | |

## Ayres Word List
### 300 Words Most Used

| **A** | be | church | **F** |
| a | because | city | far |
| about | bed | cold | feel |
| after | been | come | few |
| afternoon | before | cordially | find |
| again | believe | could | fine |
| ago | best | course | first |
| all | big | **D** | five |
| almost | board | day | for |
| also | book | dear | found |
| always | both | did | four |
| am | boy | do | Friday |
| an | build | doctor | friend |
| and | business | does | from |
| another | busy | don't | **G** |
| answer | but | down | gentleman |
| any | buy | **E** | get |
| anything | by | each | girl |
| are | **C** | eight | give |
| arrest | call | enclose | glad |
| as | can | enough | go |
| ask | cannot | even | good |
| at | car | ever | great |
| away | care | every | ground |
| **B** | cent | expect | **H** |
| back | child | eye | had |
| bad | children | | half |

hand
has
have
he
head
hear
help
her
here
him
his
home
hope
hour
house
how

**I**

I
if
in
into
is
it
its

**J**

just

**K**

keep
kind
knew
know

**L**

last

late
let
letter
life
like
little
live
long
look
love

**M**

madam
made
mail
make
man
many
May
me
mean
meet
men
mile
Miss
Monday
money
month
more
morning
most
mother
Mr.
much

must
my

**N**

need
never
new
next
nice
night
nine
no
not
nothing
now
number

**O**

oblige
o'clock
of
off
office
old
on
once
one
only
or
order
other
our
out
over
own

**P**

paper
party
pay
people
perhaps
picture
place
please
put

**Q**

quite

**R**

read
receive
respectfully
return
right
room

**S**

said
same
Saturday
say
says
school
see
seem
send
sent
shall
she
should

show

side

since

sincerely

sir

sixteen

so

some

something

soon

start

still

street

such

Sunday

sure

**T**

take

talk

tell

than

thank

that

the

their

them

then

there

these

they

thing

think

this

those

though

thought

three

through

Thursday

time

to

today

tomorrow

too

trip

truly

try

Tuesday

two

**U**

under

until

up

us

use

**V**

very

**W**

want

was

we

week

well

were

what

when

where

which

while

without

with

who

why

will

wish

word

work

write

would

**Y**

year

yesterday

yet

you

your

# Thorndike List
## First 500 Words

| | | | |
|---|---|---|---|
| a | bad | brought | cut |
| about | ball | build | dark |
| above | bank | burn | day |
| across | be | but | dead |
| add | bear | buy | dear |
| after | beautiful | by | death |
| again | became | call | deep |
| against | because | came | did |
| air | bed | can | die |
| all | been | care | do |
| almost | before | carry | does |
| alone | begin | case | done |
| along | behind | cause | door |
| also | being | certain | down |
| always | believe | change | draw |
| am | best | child | dress |
| among | better | children | drink |
| an | between | church | drive |
| and | big | city | drop |
| another | bird | clear | during |
| answer | black | close | each |
| any | blow | cold | ear |
| apple | blue | color | early |
| are | body | come | earth |
| arm | book | company | east |
| around | both | corn | eat |
| as | box | could | egg |
| ask | boy | country | end |
| at | bread | course | enough |
| away | bring | cover | even |
| back | brother | cross | ever |

| | | | |
|---|---|---|---|
| every | front | here | law |
| eye | full | high | lay |
| face | garden | hill | lead |
| fair | gave | him | learn |
| fall | general | himself | leave |
| family | get | his | left |
| far | girl | hold | length |
| fast | give | home | less |
| father | given | hope | let |
| fear | glad | horse | letter |
| feel | go | hot | lie |
| feet | God | hour | life |
| few | gold | house | light |
| field | good | how | like |
| fill | got | hundred | line |
| find | great | I | little |
| fine | green | if | live |
| fire | ground | in | long |
| first | grow | into | look |
| five | had | is | lost |
| floor | hair | it | love |
| flower | half | its | low |
| fly | hand | just | made |
| follow | happy | keep | make |
| food | hard | kill | man |
| foot | has | kind | many |
| for | have | king | mark |
| form | he | know | matter |
| found | head | known | may |
| four | hear | land | me |
| free | heart | large | mean |
| fresh | heavy | last | measure |
| friend | help | late | meet |
| from | her | laugh | men |

| | | | |
|---|---|---|---|
| might | on | reach | set |
| mile | once | read | several |
| milk | one | ready | shall |
| mind | only | reason | she |
| mine | open | receive | ship |
| miss | or | red | short |
| money | order | remain | should |
| month | other | remember | show |
| more | our | rest | side |
| morning | out | rich | sight |
| most | over | ride | silver |
| mother | own | right | since |
| mountain | paper | river | sing |
| move | part | road | sister |
| much | pass | rock | sit |
| must | pay | roll | six |
| my | people | room | sleep |
| name | person | round | small |
| near | picture | run | so |
| need | piece | said | soft |
| never | place | sail | soldier |
| new | plain | same | some |
| next | plant | save | something |
| night | play | saw | sometime |
| no | please | say | son |
| north | point | school | soon |
| not | poor | sea | sound |
| nothing | power | second | south |
| now | present | see | speak |
| number | pretty | seem | spring |
| of | put | seen | stand |
| off | quick | send | start |
| often | rain | sent | state |
| old | raise | serve | stay |

| | | | |
|---|---|---|---|
| step | they | until | while |
| still | thing | up | which |
| stone | think | upon | white |
| stop | third | us | who |
| story | this | use | whole |
| street | those | very | why |
| strong | though | visit | wide |
| such | thought | voice | will |
| summer | thousand | wait | wind |
| sun | three | walk | window |
| sure | through | wall | winter |
| sweet | till | want | wish |
| table | time | war | with |
| take | to | warm | without |
| talk | today | was | woman |
| tell | together | watch | wood |
| ten | too | water | word |
| than | top | way | work |
| thank | town | we | world |
| that | train | week | would |
| the | tree | well | write |
| their | true | went | year |
| them | try | were | yet |
| then | turn | what | you |
| there | two | when | young |
| these | under | where | your |

# Twenty Lessons Preparatory to Use of Dictionary

## Lesson I

Teacher's Note: Show alphabetically indexed blank book to class before asking questions.

What do you mean by "alphabetical"?

*Ans.* Alphabetical means in the regular order of the alphabet.

Write in your notebook the 26 letters of the alphabet in regular order.

What is an index?

*Ans.* An index is something that points out or indicates.

What do you mean by an alphabetically indexed blank book?

*Ans.* An alphabetically indexed blank book is one that has the letters of the alphabet in regular order on the edge of the pages. You write all words that begin with "a" on the pages pointed out by the letter "a" on the edge of a page. You write all words that begin with "b" on the pages pointed out by the letter "b" on the edge of a page, and so with all 26 of the letters.

Buy an indexed blank book at the ten cent store and bring to class.

### Lesson II

Study the letters on your indexed blank book.
Find quickly a, i, q, h, p, z.

Divide the blank book into thirds, as nearly as possible.

Have the pages that contain the first eight letters—a, b, c, d, e, f, g, h—in one group; those that contain the second eight letters—i, j, k, l, m, n, o, p—in the second group, and those that contain the remaining ten letters—q, r, s, t, u, v, w, x, y, z—in the last group.

Separate these groups from each other with colored cards.

Write in your notebooks the three groups of letters.

Ask a classmate to find one letter of each group on his indexed blank book.

### Lesson III

Beginning with "a," find in your word list one word beginning with each of the first eight letters in the alphabet—a, b, c, d, e, f, g, h—and write on proper page in indexed blank book.

### Lesson IV

Beginning with "i," find in your word list one word beginning with each of the second eight letters of the alphabet—i, j, k, l, m, n, o, p—and write on proper page in indexed blank book.

### Lesson V

Beginning with "q," find in your word list one word beginning with each of the last ten letters in the alphabet—q, r, s, t, u, v, w, x, y, z—and write on proper page in indexed blank book.

## Lesson VI

Teacher's Note: Divide several words into syllables orally. Write the words on the board with a hyphen between the syllables. Ask pupils to divide words into syllables orally, then to write them in notebooks, using hyphens in the proper places.

What is a syllable?

*Ans.* A syllable is that part of a word that can be distinctly uttered with one effort of the voice; as, ba-by.

What is a hyphen?

*Ans.* A hyphen is a mark ( - ) used to separate, or join, two syllables.

Teacher's Note: Explain use of hyphen at end of lines.

In your indexed blank book, add two words, beginning with the proper letters, to each page of first group of eight letters—a, b, c, d, e, f, g, h.

Divide these words into syllables.

## Lesson VII

In your indexed blank book, add two two-syllable words, beginning with the proper letters to each page of the second group of eight letters —i, j, k, l, m, n, o, p.

Divide these words into syllables.

## Lesson VIII

In your indexed blank book, add two two-syllable words, beginning with the proper letters, to each page of the third group of ten letters— q, r, s, t, u, v, w, x, y, z.

Divide these words into syllables.

## Lesson IX

Teacher's Note: Accent several words for pupils, asking them to tell you which syllable you made more prominent than the rest in each word.
Ask them to choose words in their readers and tell which syllable is most prominent in each. Show them the accent mark.

What do you mean by "accent"?

*Ans.* Accent is the stress laid by the voice upon a particular syllable of a word, so as to make it more prominent than the rest; as, mon'-ey.

Write in your note books six words of two or three syllables.

Place the accent mark on the proper syllables.

## Lesson X

In your indexed blank book, add four words with two or three syllables to each page in the first group of eight letters—a, b, c, d, e, f, g, h.

Divide each word into syllables and place accent mark.

## Lesson XI

In your indexed blank book, add four words with two or three syllables to each page in the second group of eight letters—i, j, k, l, m, n, o, p.

Divide each word into syllables and place accent.

## Lesson XII

In your indexed blank book, add four words with two or three syllables to each page in the third group of ten letters—q, r, s, t, u, v, w, x, y, z.

Divide each word into syllables and place accent.

## Lesson XIII

Teacher's Note: Call pupils' attention to the fact that they now have, in their indexed blank books, seven words, beginning with the proper letter, under each letter of the alphabet.

Explain that these words are in alphabetical order, according to the first letter only. Explain that you wish them put in "exact alphabetical order," as soon as the pupil has learned to do this, because that is the way they are put in the dictionary. Show what you mean by "exact alphabetical order." Use very simple examples, until the meaning is clear cab, can, cap, car, cat.

Show that words are put in exact alphabetical order in the dictionary, in order that they may be found more quickly.

Write in your notebooks the words, "all," "ago," "also," "about." Then, write each of these words on a separate slip of paper. Put the slips in what you believe to be exact alphabetical order. Then number the slips and copy the words in your notebook in the exact alphabetical order. For these four words, the order should be: 1. about. 2. ago. 3. all. 4. also.

If you do not understand this, ask your teacher to explain it again.

## Lesson XIV

Write in your notebooks the words, "best," "back," "book," "bed." Then, write each of these words on a separate slip of paper. Change the position of the slips, until you think you have the words in exact alphabetical order. Then number the slips and copy the words in your note book in the proper order.

For these four words, the order should be: 1. back. 2. bed. 3. best. 4. book.

## Lesson XV

Write in your notebooks the words, "could," "call," "city," "church," "children." Then write each of these words on a separate slip of paper.

Change the position of the slips until you think you have the words in exact alphabetical order. Then number the slips and copy the words in your notebook in the order in which you have numbered them. Ask your teacher to see if you have placed them in exact alphabetical order.

### Lesson XVI

Find in your indexed blank book the seven words you have written on the page labeled "A." Write these seven words on seven separate slips. Change the position of the slips until you have the words in exact alphabetical order. Then number the words. Copy them, in the order in which you have numbered them, in your indexed blank book, on the page opposite the one on which you first wrote them. Ask your teacher to see if the words are in exact alphabetical order.

### Lesson XVII

Find in your indexed blank book the seven words you have written on the page labeled "B." Write these seven words on seven separate slips. Change the position of the slips until you have the words in exact alphabetical order. Then number the words. Copy them, in the order in which you have numbered them, in your indexed blank book, on the page opposite the one on which you first wrote them. Ask your teacher to see if the words are in exact alphabetical order.

## Lesson XVIII

Find in your indexed blank book the seven words you have written on the page labeled "C." Write these seven words on seven separate slips. Change the position of the slips until you have the words in exact alphabetical order. Then number the words. Copy them, in the order in which you have numbered them, in your indexed blank book, on the page opposite the one on which you first wrote them. Ask your teacher to see if the words are in exact alphabetical order.

## Lesson XIX

Find in your indexed blank book the seven words you have written on the page labeled "D." Write these seven words on seven separate slips. Change the position of the slips until you have the words in exact alphabetical order. Then number the words. Copy them, in the order in which you have numbered them, in your indexed blank book, on the page opposite the one on which you first wrote them. Ask your teacher to see if the words are in exact alphabetical order.

## Lesson XX

Find in your indexed blank book the seven words you have written on the page labeled "E." Write these seven words on seven separate slips. Change the position of the slips until you have the words in exact alphabetical order. Then number the words. Copy them, in the order in which you have numbered them, in your indexed blank book, on the page opposite the one on which you first wrote them. Ask your teacher to see if the words are in exact alphabetical order.

### Follow Up Work

Continue, as home or seat work, until you have arranged in exact alphabetical order all twenty-six of your groups of words in your indexed blank books.

Continue adding new words that you wish to remember under each of the twenty-six letters until you have filled all the blank pages under each letter in your indexed blank books.

# Writing
# First Twenty-Lesson Course

Teacher's Note: Drill on writing pupil's name and address at each lesson, beginning with the first lesson.

## Lessons I and II

## Lessons III, IV, and V

## Lessons VI, VII, and VIII

### Lessons IX, X, and XI

### Lesson XII

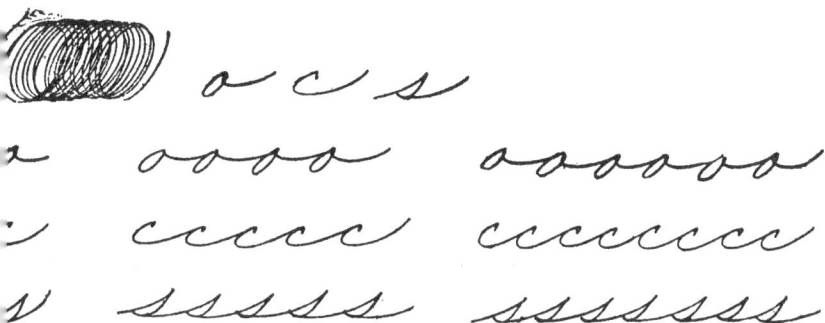

## Lesson XIII

*ba ba ba   bo bo bo*
*be be be   bi bi bi*
*bu bu bu   br br br*

## Lesson XIV

*om om om   on on on*
*oh oh oh   ob ob ob*
*of of of   og og og*
*ov ov ov   ox ox ox*

## Lesson XV

*va va va vo vo vo*

*vi vi vi ve ve ve*

*vu vu vu vr vr vr*

*T T X K*

*T T T T   F F F F*

*X X X X   K K K K*

## Lesson XVI

*wa wa wa wo wo wo*

*wi wi wi we we we*

*wu wu wu wu*

*wr wr wr wr*

*m m m m M N U V*

*m m m m N N N N*

*U U U U   V V V V V*

## Lesson **XVII**

*wr wr wr wr*
*wh wh wh wh*
*tr tr tr tr*
*th th th th*

*W X Y Z*
*W W W W X X X X*
*Y Y Y Y Z Z Z Z*

## Lesson **XVIII**

*O O O O E G O E D*
*E E E E E G G G G*
*O O O O O E E E E*
*D D D D G O E*

## Lesson XIX

## Lesson XX

(This sentence contains all the letters of the alphabet.)

Find how many small and capital letters you can recognize immediately.

Find how many small letters you can write from dictation.

# Writing
## Second Twenty-Lesson Course

Note: In all lessons work for correct spacing, height and slant.

**Lesson I**

*Illinois Indiana*
*Inn Ink Iowa*
*I want to write.*
*I will use my arm.*

## Lesson II

*J J J J J*
*J J J J J J J J J*

*Joined Joy Joining*
*Jane Jamestown*
*James Inman June*
*Join letters with an*
*easy movement.*

## Lesson III

*G G G G  G G G G*
*G G G G  Good*
*Gain  Georgia*
*Gained Graceful*
*Good enough is*
*not enough.*
*Gaining in writing.*

## Lesson IV

*S S S S   S S S S*
*S S S S   Swim*
*Statement Swan*
*Swimming State*
*Scranton Summer*
*Slant Size Spacing*

## Lesson V

11111  4444  666
777  999  1414  7979

222  333  555
888  000  3535  6262
1234567890 $ ¢ #

## Lesson VI

OOOOO DDDD
DDDD DDDDD
Delaware Doris
Dominion Delivery
Domino Dear Delia
Don't neglect the
ending stroke.

## Lesson VII

H H H H   H H H
Hike Hand Harris
Harrison Helene
K K K K   K K K
King Kind Kin
Kentucky Katie K
Knowledge of letter
forms is essential.

## Lesson VIII

*2 2 2   2 2 2   2 2*

*2 2 2 2   2 2 2 2*

*Queen Quality Que*

*Queer   Queenstown*

*Quebec is in Canada.*

*Quitters never win.*

## Lesson IX

*F F   F F   F F*

*F F   F F   F F*

*Franklin Fame*

*Fannie Finished*

*Fourth Five Fan*

*Free arm movement*

## Lesson X

*mmmm M M M M*
*M M M M M M M M*
*Miles Mine My*
*Mink Montana*
*Muscular Movement*

## Lesson XI

*J J J J J J J J*
*J J J J J J J J*
*Tillie Tennessee*
*Try This Train*

*The quick brown fox*
*jumps over the lazy dog.*

## Lesson XII

W W W W  W W W
W W W W  Will
Washington Wins
Woodrow Wilson
Willie Work Willingly
Winter William W

## Lesson XIII

O E E E E E E E E
E E E E E  E E E E
Evanston Every
Easy Exercises and
Earnest Endeavor E
Each one brings one

## Lesson XIV

RRRR RRRR

River Run Rare

Richmond Ring

Robert E. Lee Review

Ruth R Robertson

PPPPP Position

Practice Perseverance

Promotion! P. B. Remsen

Robert A. Parmer R

## Lesson XV

*Oaaa aaaa*
*aaaa aaaa*

*Annum Accent*
*Autumn Again*
*Attain Awards*
*As a man aims A*
*America is a land*
*of opportunity*

## Lesson XVI

147147147  444  77;
96969696  8888  000(
23232323  5555  33;
1234567890  75937546

## Lesson XVII

*B B B B     B B B B*
*B B B B     B B B B*

*Baltimore Better*
*Balloon Building*
*Brave Bob Band*
*Bobbin Borrow*
*Bulletin Barber*

## Lesson XVIII

*L L L L   L L L L*
*L L L L   L L L L*

*Link   Land   Louis*
*Letters   Lillian   Lou*
*Louisiana   Lincoln*

*Let us have faith that*
*right makes might and*
*in that faith, let us to*
*the end do our duty as we*
*see it*  Abraham Lincoln

## Lesson XIX

*Columbus Count*

*Certificate Combines*

*Cinnamon Course*

*Confidence is the*
*secret of strength.*

## Lesson XX

*O O O    Orleans*

*U U U    Uniontown*

*V V V    Virginia*

*X X X    Xenia*

*Z Z Z    Zanesville*

*Ocean Zion Vera*

*Universe Xerxes*

*New York is the largest city in the United States.*

Review all capitals.

# English
## First Twenty-Lesson Course

### Letter Writing

Teacher's Note: The aim, in oral English, of this Twenty-Lesson Course is to enable the pupil to speak more freely, correctly, and interestingly, and to be able to give three or four correct sentences on one subject. Use a few minutes of each English period for oral English.

The aim, in written English, is to enable pupil to write correctly a very simple personal letter and a simple business letter; to fill out necessary business forms, as money orders, checks, and receipts; to wrap and address a package for mailing.

### Lesson I

Bring to class a picture or a poster.

In three or four sentences, tell the class why you think it is interesting.

Teacher's Note: As each pupil talks, tactfully help him with pronunciation, language forms and in complete modes of expression.

### Lesson II

Copy your name, write it from dictation, write it from memory.

Practice on this until you can write it with ease and without error.

### Lesson III

Copy in your notebook the first sentence in your reading lesson. The words in this lesson are printed. When you write them they will be in script. Change the words in your word list lesson from print to script.

### Lesson IV

Find in your reading book five words that begin with capital letters.

Write these words in your notebook.

Tell why each one begins with a capital.

Whenever you find a word that begins with a capital, write it in your notebook. If you do not know why it begins with a capital, ask your teacher to tell you.

### Lesson V

Copy in your notebook two sentences from your reader.

Put a period or a question mark after each one, just as it is in the reader.

### Lesson VI

Write in your notebook two sentences that should be followed by a period.

### Lesson VII

Write in your notebook two sentences that should be followed by a question mark.

### Lesson VIII

Write in your notebook two short sentences that ask a question of your teacher. Put a question mark after these sentences.

### Lesson IX

Write in your notebook the following abbreviations. Put a period after each one. Write

out in full the word for which each abbreviation
stands:

| Mr. | St. | S. C. |
| Mrs. | Ave. | Ark. |
| Dr. | N. C. | Ala. |

### Lesson X

Copy one of the following letters in your notebook:

> Little Rock, Arkansas,
> Oct. 12, 1934.

Dear Miss White:

Please excuse Mary for being absent from
school.  She was sick.

> Sincerely yours,
> Mary Little.

> Rock Hill, S. C.,
> Oct. 12, 1934.

Dear Mother:

Can't you possibly come down for a visit next
week?  The baby is so cunning now that I do
want you to see her.

When her father came home from work yesterday she took two steps by herself and tumbled
right into his arms.  When he says, "Give Dad
some sugar," she holds her little mouth up to
be kissed every time.  You just must come and
see her before she loses her cunning little ways.

> With dearest love,
> Betty.

### Lesson XI

Turn to the letter that you copied in Lesson X. Draw a red line under the date line, a blue line under the salutation, a black line under the body of the letter, a green line under the complimentary close, and a yellow line under your signature.

Notice that each of these parts has a regular place of its own.

### Lesson XII

Copy in your notebook the following personal letter:

Fairhope, Alabama,<br>December 20, 1934.

Dear John:

We are certainly glad to hear that you and your family are coming back here to live.

You will hardly know the old town, but all the new things, like the paved streets, the bright lights, the fine school building, the free library, and the new bank, will just suit an up-to-date man like you. And we can use you in half a dozen different places.

Let me know if I can be of any help when you are ready to come.

Your old friend,

Will.

Look through it carefully, with the teacher, to see if you have made any errors.

Correct the errors and copy again.

Continue to correct and copy your letter until there are no errors in it.

Teacher's Note: Only correct practice makes perfect.

## Lesson XIII

Write a simple letter that your teacher will dictate to you.

Look through it carefully, with the teacher, to see if you have made any errors.

Correct the errors and copy again.

Continue to correct and copy this letter that you have written from dictation until there are no errors in it.

## Lesson XIV

Bring an envelope to class.  Address it to a friend.

Write a short letter to this friend.  In the letter tell him about Adult Schools. Look through the letter carefully, with the teacher, to see if you have made any errors.

Correct the errors and copy the letter.

Continue to correct and copy your letter until there are no errors in it.  Then mail the letter to your friend.

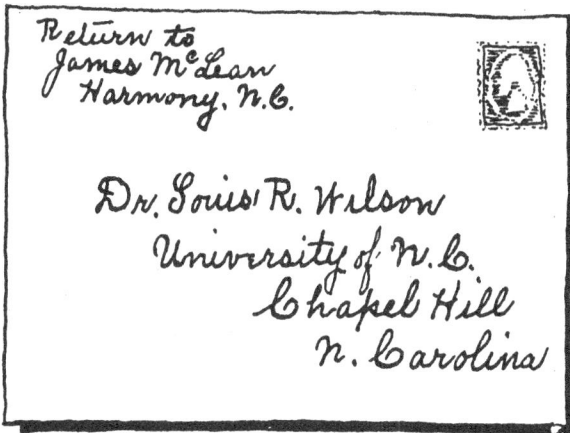

## Lesson XV

Bring to class an advertisement, a sign, and a joke.

In three or four sentences, tell the class why you think they are good.

## Lesson XVI

Copy in your notebook the following business letter:

531 Broad Street,
Asheville, N C.,
May 31, 1934.

High Point Furniture Factory,
High Point, N. C.

Gentlemen:

In reply to your advertisement in today's "News" for a cabinet maker, I wish to apply for the position.

I have worked for six years in the cabinet room of the Asheville Furniture Company, and believe you would find my work satisfactory.

I refer you, by permission, to Mr. J. E. Melton, Superintendent of the Asheville Furniture Factory.

Very truly yours,

Arthur Stone.

Draw a red line under the date line, a blue line under the salutation, a black line under the body of the letter, a green line under the complimentary close, and a yellow line under your signature. Then draw a purple line under the only part that is left. This will be the business address of the firm to whom the letter is written.

### Lesson XVII

Copy in your notebook the following business letter:

Raleigh, N. C.,
June 8, 1934.

Boone Hardware Co.,
Selma, Ala.

Gentlemen:

Enclosed you will find a check for $32.54. Please send me by freight:

| | |
|---|---|
| 1 Albany Cook Stove. . . . . . . . . | $20.00 |
| 1 Poppy 6 qt. Churn . . . . . . . . | 7.50 |
| 3 doz. Exhibit Fruit Jars. . . . . | 4.80 |
| 6 Excel. Fishing Lines No. 20. . | .60 |
| Fish hooks Nos. 1-8 assorted. . . | .30 |
| | $33.20 |
| Less 2% disc. . . . . . . . . . | $32.54 |

Very truly yours,

S. W. Minton.

Look through it carefully, with the teacher, to see if you have made any errors.

Correct the errors and copy again.

Continue to correct and copy the letter until there are no errors in it.

### Lesson XVIII

Fill out a money order blank.

Write a check and endorse one.

Make out a receipt.

Paste these forms in your notebook so that you will have them for reference.

Wrap and address a package for mailing.

Teacher's Note: The package may be wrapped and addressed at home and brought to class for inspection and correction.

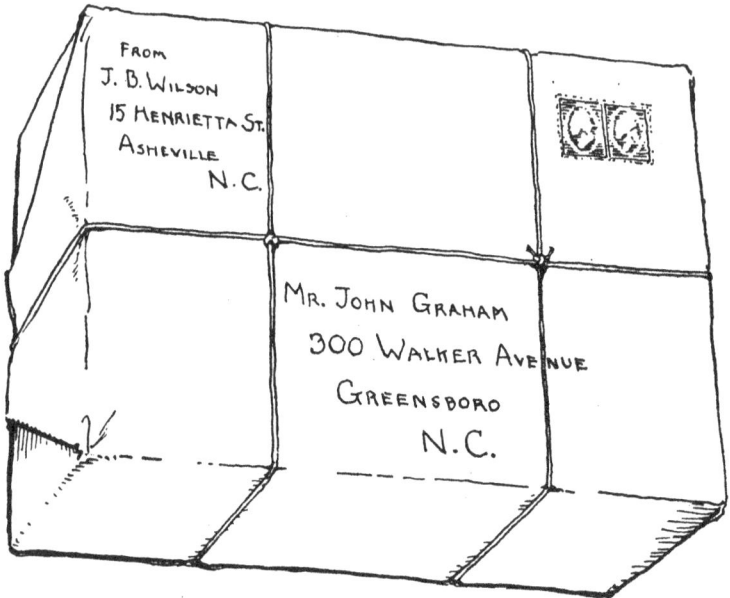

## Lesson XIX

Bring an envelope to class.

Address it to a business firm whose advertisement you have.

Write them a letter, asking that they send you the article advertised.   Enclose money order or check, if necessary.

Teacher's Note:  Bring to class advertisements from many reliable firms, offering free samples or very inexpensive articles.   Put on the board the address of some of the State and Federal Departments and ask pupils to order interesting bulletins from them.

## Lesson XX

In three or four sentences, welcome a distinguished visitor to your term closing exercises.

In three or four more sentences, introduce him to the class.

Teacher's Note: At the term closing exercises, ask half a dozen pupils to give some of the best three-sentence themes that have been worked out in class.

# English
# Second Twenty-Lesson Course

## Lesson I

Bring to class a poster or picture on Health.

In a few sentences, tell the class why you think it is a good poster or picture.

Discuss with the class a number of other Health posters or pictures.

Get from these posters as many ideas 'on health as possible. Think over the ideas you have always had on health.

Then write correctly a paragraph of eight or nine sentences on Health.

Teacher's Note: Bring to class at least a dozen Health posters.

## Lesson II

Read one of *Aesop's Fables,* or one of the *Stories of Great Americans* or one of the *Fifty Famous Stories Retold.*

Think over what you consider the most interesting and most important parts of the story. Tell the story to the class.

## Lesson III

Find in a newspaper or magazine eight words that begin with capital letters. Tell why they begin with capitals. Use these words in sentences of your own.

### Lesson IV

Copy in your notebook the following sentences that tell when capitals are used. Copy the example of each. Write another example of each use of capitals.

A capital letter is used for:

The first word in every sentence; as, "Bread is the staff of life."

The first word of every line of poetry; as,

"Speak gently; it is better far
To rule by love than fear."

The names of people and places; as, Robt. E. Lee, Virginia.

The words I and O; as, "I came, I saw, I conquered," and "Be glad, O ye righteous."

The days of the week and the months of the year; as, Sunday, October. Holidays; as, Christmas, Thanksgiving.

The names of God; as, Jesus Christ, Jehovah, Lord.

The first word of a formal quotation; as, "Judge not that ye be not judged."

### Lesson V

Find, in your reader, sentences that illustrate two different uses of the period.

Write in your notebook two original sentences that illustrate these two uses of the period.

Find in your notebook a sentence that illustrates the use of the question mark.

Write in your notebook an original sentence that illustrates the use of the question mark.

Copy the following sentences that tell when the period and the question mark are used:

A period is placed:

After a declarative (telling) sentence; as, "Wise parents are a child's best asset."

After an imperative (commanding) sentence as, "Pay your taxes."

After abbreviations; as, Mr.

The question mark is used after an interrogative sentence (one that asks a question); as, "Did you have an exhibit at the fair?"

## Lesson VI

Find in your reader:

1. An exclamation point.
2. A hyphen.
3. A comma.
4. An apostrophe.

Copy in your notebook the sentences in which you found these punctuation marks.

## Lesson VII

Copy in your notebook the following sentences that tell when to use the exclamation point, the hyphen, the comma, and the apostrophe:

The exclamation point is used after an exclamation (a sentence of strong feeling); as, "Run for your life!"

The hyphen is used:

To divide compound words; as, worn-out.

To divide words at the end of a line; as, baby.

The comma is used in a sentence when a pause is needed; as, "Yes, I saw her."

The apostrophe is used:

To show possession; as, Mary's lamb.

To show that letters are left out of certain words; as, don't.

Teacher's Note: Teach use of colon and quotation marks through observation. But have uses copied in notebooks.

The colon is used:

After the salutation in a letter-heading; as, Dear Sir:

Before a formal quotation; as, Patrick Henry said: "Give me liberty or give me death."

Quotation marks are used to enclose the exact words of another person; as, He said, "Be joyful."

### Lesson VIII

Copy in your notebook the following verbs, with the headings above:

| Today<br>Present | Yesterday<br>Past | Use the verbs in this column with am, is, are, was, were, have, has, or had. |
|---|---|---|
| 1. do | did | done |
| 2. sing | sang | sung |
| 3. ring | rang | rung |
| 4. eat | ate | eaten |
| 5. see | saw | seen |
| 6. take | took | taken |
| 7. come | came | come |
| 8. write | wrote | written |

Write in your notebook the following sentences that give drill on one of the above verbs:

1. I see your new radio set.
2. I saw it yesterday.
3. I had not seen it before.

Write in your notebook three sentences that give drill on the verb "take," "took," "taken."

## Lesson IX

Copy the following sentences, using the correct word. When you are not sure which is the correct word, look it up in the list in Lesson VIII.

1. I (took, taken) an apple.
2. I (have saw, have seen) you many times.
3. He (taken, took) it before I (seen, saw) him.
4. They (have come, have came) to see you.
5. Have you (wrote, written) your lesson?
6. Have you (saw, seen) the picture?

## Lesson X

Tell the class, in a two or three minute talk, the most interesting experience you have had this month. Or, tell them the most interesting experience of which you have heard or read.

## Lesson XI

Write, from dictation, the following sentences:

1. The children are well.
2. I am going to Washington next Monday.
3. Please answer this letter as soon as you can.

4. Please excuse Tom's absence yesterday.

5. Have you read your new magazine?

6. Mr. Robert Miller and Miss Jane Gray were married last night.

Look through these sentences, comparing them with those in the book, to see if you have made any errors.

Correct the errors and copy the sentences correctly.

Write the sentences again from dictation. Find and correct all errors.

Continue to write from dictation and to correct until there are no errors.

Teacher's Note: Give at least two or three sentences from dictation in each English lesson. Much of the correcting and re-writing can be done at home.

### Lesson XII

Write, from dictation, the following quotations:

Do the duty that lies nearest thee.—Goethe.

Breathes there a man with soul so dead,
Who never to himself hath said,
"This is my own, my native land!"—Scott.

This above all: To thine own self be true,
And it must follow, as the night the day,
Thou canst not then be false to any man.
—Shakespeare.

Correct any errors you may make and re-write correctly.

Continue to take from dictation and to correct until there are no errors.

## Lesson XIII

Write from dictation the following paragraph:

The words "house" and "home" are often confused. The home expresses the family life within the house. The house is the place where the home maker gathers furnishing to make the home more comfortable and beautiful. Here the home maker works out standards of living, holds up ideals before her family, all of which aid in creating the beautiful "home spirit," which we talk about. All home makers should recognize the fact that a house may be elegantly equipped and furnished, may have every convenience and comfort, and yet fail to be a "home." Whether it is to be a home, not simply a house, depends largely upon the home maker.

Correct any errors you may make and re-write correctly. Continue to take from dictation and to correct until there are no errors.

## Lesson XIV

Write a short letter to one of the County or City officials, telling him about the Adult Schools. Ask him to visit your school.

Find and correct all errors. When you have made a copy without an error, mail it to the official.

## Lesson XV

Prepare a three minute talk on "Recreation in My Community."

Before making the talk, make a recreation survey of your community, using the following outline:

1. Importance.
2. Kinds of recreation in community now.
3. Number of social gatherings held there last year.
4. Number of books in the community.
5. Number of telephones.
6. Number of automobiles.
7. Number of magazines and newspapers subscribed for regularly in the community.
8. Kinds of music that may be heard there.
9. Recreations you would like to see there, both for children and grown-ups.
10. Plans for securing these recreations.

Teacher's Note: Discuss with the class the following simple standards for a good speaker. Ask them to copy these standards in their notebooks and to learn them.

Write this outline in your notebook.

### Standards for a Good Speaker

Position:
Stand straight.
Voice:
Speak distinctly.
Style:
Watch your English.
Use short sentences.
Make it interesting.
Ideas:
a. Begin with an interesting sentence to make people listen.
b. End with a thought that they will remember.

A pupil expressed it this way: "Put a good sentence first to make people listen. Put a good sentence last to leave a good taste in the mouth."

### Lesson XVI

Discuss with your teacher and the class a number of good newspapers and magazines. Decide which newspaper and which magazine you like best.

Write a letter, subscribing for the newspaper or the magazine. If you have the money to spare, enclose a money order or check, and mail the letter.

### Lesson XVII

Read everything you can find in your reader about "Citizenship" or about "Proper Food." Read everything you can find in magazines on the subject you choose. Talk with wise people about it. Get together all the pictures you can find on the subject. Find out if anybody knows any jokes on your subject. Think over everything that has come in your experience that has any connection with your subject. Then write a paragraph of eight or nine sentences and you will be surprised how interesting it will be.

Write this paragraph in your notebook. Correct all of the errors that you can find. Ask the teacher to correct all of the errors that she can find. Write the paragraph again. Continue to correct and write again until there are no errors.

Teacher's Note: Other subjects to suggest for topics or paragraphs: Thrift and Education.

## Lesson XVIII

Read one of *Aesop's Fables,* or one of the
*Stories of Great Americans* or one of the *Fifty*

*Famous Stories Retold.* Tell the story to the class as well as you can. Write in your notebook the most important and the most interesting parts of the story.

Correct all of the errors that you can find. Ask the teacher to correct all of the errors that she can find. Write your story again. Continue to correct and write again until there are no errors.

### Lesson XIX

Study two good pictures with your teacher. Write from her dictation a paragraph of five or six sentences about each.

Correct all of the errors that you can find. Ask the teacher to correct all of the errors that she can find. Write your paragraphs again. Continue to correct and write again until there are no errors. When you have written the paragraphs correctly, paste a small copy of the picture below them.

### Lesson XX

Make a three minute talk at your Term Closing Exercises. Prove by this talk that you have learned to speak more freely, correctly, and interestingly. Remember the Standards of a Good Speaker.

Teacher's Note: Five fine results of working steadily for a high standard of correctness are:
1. Pupils become dissatisfied with slip-shod work.
2. They have active desire for definite improvement.
3. They become interested in self-criticism.
4. They welcome teacher's suggestions for plans to progress.
5. They do progress.

# Arithmetic
# First Twenty Lessons

Teacher's Note: These lessons are to be used when reading ability has been developed. Part of the work is to be done at home each time and part in class in a notebook which the pupil will keep for reference.

Give pupil drill on reading the following phrases and parts of sentences:

| | |
|---|---|
| How much | If a man earns |
| How many | If a woman earns |
| Find the cost of | Make numbers |
| A man paid | How much can he save |
| A woman paid | How much can she save |
| If it costs | How much change should be given |

## Lesson I

## Addition

Type examples:

| Addition—3 | 12 | 12 | 106 | 269 |
|---|---|---|---|---|
| 2 | 3 | 13 | 121 | 122 |
| 5 | 15 | 25 | 227 | 391 |

Make numbers from 1 to 100. Number pages in notebook. Copy calendar.

Note: When we add numbers above 10, we write them under each other. We must keep the right side even and put the figures exactly under each other. We then add each column separately, always beginning on the right.

Teach and

| Add: | Add: |
|---|---|
| 24 | 40 |
| 23 | 25 |
| 47 | 65 |
| The sum is 47 | The sum is 65 |

[ 109 ]

Add:

| Cows | Sheep | Calves | Horses |
|------|-------|--------|--------|
| 24   | 46    | 48     | 40     |
| 23   | 21    | 31     | 25     |

| Goats | Chickens | Turkeys | Hogs |
|-------|----------|---------|------|
| 123   | 265      | 104     | 674  |
| 141   | 102      | 234     | 123  |

A boy bought skates for 60 cents and a ball for 21 cents. How much did he pay for both?

| Add 10 to each of these numbers. Put sum on line | These 3 examples give drill on combination of 10 with other numbers |
|---|---|
| 1——— | 7   5   5 |
| 2——— | 5   2   1 |
| 3——— | 2   2   2 |
| 4——— | 3   6   7 |
| 5——— | |
| 6——— | |
| 7——— | |
| 8——— | |
| 9——— | |

## Lesson II

### Addition

Drill on 8 of the basic addition combinations and put in notebooks.

| 2 | 3 | 4 | 5 | 6 | 7 | 8 | 9 |
|---|---|---|---|---|---|---|---|
| 2 | 2 | 2 | 2 | 2 | 2 | 2 | 2 |

Add 2 to each of the numbers below:

| 2 12 | 4 14 | 3 13 | 10 40 | 5 15 |
|------|------|------|-------|------|
| 6 36 | 9 29 | 7 57 | 8 78 | |

Make numbers by 2's to 24.

Note 1.  When the figures in the first column amount to 10 or more, only the right hand figure is put down.  The left hand figure is carried over to the next column.

Note 2. Dollars must be written under dollars, and cents under cents.  The point separates dollars from cents.  The points must fall under each other.

Add:

```
28      8 + 8 = 16
48      Put down 6 and carry the 1 over
76      to next column.
        4 + 2 + 1 = 7      The sum is 76.
```

```
$ 4.20   3 + 5 + 0 = 8
  5.35   2 + 3 + 2 = 7
  6.23   6 + 5 + 4 = 15
$15.78      The sum is $15.78
```

Add:

| Apples | Pears | Peaches | Plums | $4.20 |
|--------|-------|---------|-------|-------|
| 28 | 36 | 49 | 28 | 5.35 |
| 38 | 26 | 39 | 66 | 6.23 |

| | | | |
|---|---|---|---|
| 6 | 8 | 7 | These examples give drill on |
| 2 | 3 | 6 | the combination of 9 with |
| 4 | 2 | 1 | other numbers. |
| 3 | 4 | 2 | |

Add 9 to each number and put result on line.

| 8—— | 9—— | 5—— | 3—— |
|------|------|------|------|
| 7—— | 6—— | 2—— | 4—— |

Jim has 7 calves, Tom has 8 and John has 16. How many have they altogether?

### Lesson III

Addition

Drill on:

| 3 | 4 | 5 | 6 | 7 | 8 | 9 |
|---|---|---|---|---|---|---|
| 3 | 3 | 3 | 3 | 3 | 3 | 3 |

Add 3 to each of the numbers below:

3 23    5 65    4 34    7 27    10 60    8 18
6 56    9 29

Make numbers by 3's to 36.

Remember to write dollars under dollars and cents under cents.

Add:

| | | | | |
|---|---|---|---|---|
| $1.25 | | | | |
| .10 | | | | |
| .75 | 194 | 636 | 160 | 104 |
| 1.00 | 249 | 248 | 342 | 296 |
| .05 | | | | |
| .50 | | | | |
| $3.65 | | | | |

A man paid $1.25 for flour, 10 cents for soda, 75 cents for meal, $1.00 for sugar, 5 cents for salt, and 50 cents for meat. How much did he pay for all?

**Lesson IV**

Addition

Drill on:

| 4 | 5 | 6 | 7 | 8 | 9 |
|---|---|---|---|---|---|
| 4 | 4 | 4 | 4 | 4 | 4 |

Add 4 to these numbers:

4 14   7 27   5 75   9 29   6 26   8 28

Make numbers by 4's to 48.
Make numbers by 5's to 60.

Find the amount of the following bills:

| | | | |
|---|---|---|---|
| Hat .......... | $ 3.28 | Sugar ........ | $ .50 |
| Dress ........ | 12.42 | Flour ......... | .98 |
| Shoes ........ | 5.00 | Meat ......... | 1.25 |
| Hose ........ | 1.98 | Apples ........ | .12 |
| | | Oranges ....... | .24 |

Prove by adding from top to bottom of column.

If I spend $10.00 a week for board, $.84 for car fare, $.50 for pleasure, and put $.50 in church, how much do I spend each week?

## Lesson V

Teacher's Note: Have pupils read and write numbers of three or four places.

Drill on:

| | | | | |
|---|---|---|---|---|
| 5 | 6 | 7 | 8 | 9 |
| 5 | 5 | 5 | 5 | 5 |

Add 5 to each of the numbers below:

5 15   9 29   6 46   8 28   10 80   7 37

Make numbers by 6's to 12.
Make numbers by 7's to 84.

A man paid $750.00 for an automobile and $84.00 for a cow. How much did he pay for both?

The postman delivered 185 letters on Monday, 286 on Tuesday, 219 on Wednesday and 227 on Thursday. How many letters did he deliver in the four days? How many did you write?

## Lesson VI

### Addition

Drill on:

| 6 | 7 | 8 | 9 |
|---|---|---|---|
| 6 | 6 | 6 | 6 |

Add 6 to each of the numbers below:

    6 16    10 70    7 47    9 29    8 38

Make numbers by 8's to 96.

Take these numbers from dictation and add:

| 7865 people | $ .48 | $4.86 |
|---|---|---|
| 4897 people | .84 | 7.57 |
| 3206 people | .75 | 4.35 |
| 4060 people | .68 | 6.95 |

If a man pays $2.20 for a shirt, $3.35 for a hat and $6.00 for shoes, how much does he pay for all?

Find the total County tax per $100.00 valuation:

    General fund ............... .08
    Road and Bridge fund....... .09
    Interest and bond fund...... .18
    Retiring bonds ........... .10
    School building, etc. ........ .05
    Teachers' salary .......... .30

**Lesson VII**

Addition

Drill on:

| 7 | 8 | 9 |
|---|---|---|
| 7 | 7 | 7 |

Add 7 to each of the numbers below:

7 17    10 90    8 58    9 39

Make numbers by 9's to 108.
Make numbers by 10's to 120.

Use these three examples to give drill on combination of 9 with other numbers:

| 6 | 6 | 7 |
|---|---|---|
| 4 | 4 | 1 |
| 3 | 2 | 2 |
| 2 | 3 | 6 |

A woman paid $12.46 for corn, $15.75 for strawberries, $9.40 for potatoes and $10.00 for chickens. How much did she pay for all?

A man paid $13.40 for groceries, $12.35 for house rent, $3.75 for water and lights and $8.45 for other expenses. How much did it all cost him?

A woman paid $2.75 for milk, $3.00 for butter and $1.50 for eggs. What did she pay for all?

## Lesson VIII

### Addition

Teacher's Note: Have pupil read and write miscellaneous numbers to 10,000.

Drill on:

```
   8          9          9
   8          8          9
  ___        ___        ___
```

Add 8 to each of the numbers below:

8 18        9 49        8 38        10 60

Make numbers by 11's to 132.
Make numbers by 12's to 144.

A man sold 3 lots. For one he received $695.00; for another, $734.00 and for the third, $392.00. How much did he receive for all?

Mr. Reed worked 193 hours, Mr. W. 187 hours, Mr. Roberts 179 hours, Mr. Taylor 125 hours a month. How many hours did all four men work?

James pays $17.50 for a suit, $2.00 for a sweater, $2.48 for a hat, $5.80 for shoes and $0.63 for a tie. How much did the outfit cost?

Add:

```
$324.53
  63.16          Prove.  Make an original
 103.34          problem in addition.
 247.66
 _____
```

## Lesson IX

### Subtraction

Type examples in Subtraction:

| 154 | 154 | 154 | 150 | 200 |
|-----|-----|-----|-----|-----|
| 41  | 92  | 85  | 85  | 85  |
| 113 | 62  | 69  | 65  | 115 |

Drill on the following basic subtraction facts:

| 4 | 5 | 6 | 7 | 8 | 9 |
|---|---|---|---|---|---|
| 2 | 2 | 3 | 4 | 4 | 6 |
|   | 3 | 2 | 3 | 3 | 3 |
|   |   | 4 | 2 | 5 | 4 |
|   |   |   | 5 | 2 | 5 |
|   |   |   |   | 6 | 7 |

Subtract 2 from each of the numbers below:

| 2 12  | 9 39 | 5 65 | 10 20 | 4 14 |
|-------|------|------|-------|------|
| 10 70 | 7 87 | 8 28 |       |      |

23 from 46

46
23
23

23 from 46 = 23.

20 from 55

55
20
35

20 from 55 = 35.

Subtract:

| Desks | Pencils | Pens | Books | Tables |
|-------|---------|------|-------|--------|
| 46    | 55      | 325  | 263   | 398    |
| 23    | 20      | 121  | 101   | 124    |

If you have 86 cents and spend 24 cents, how much will you have left?

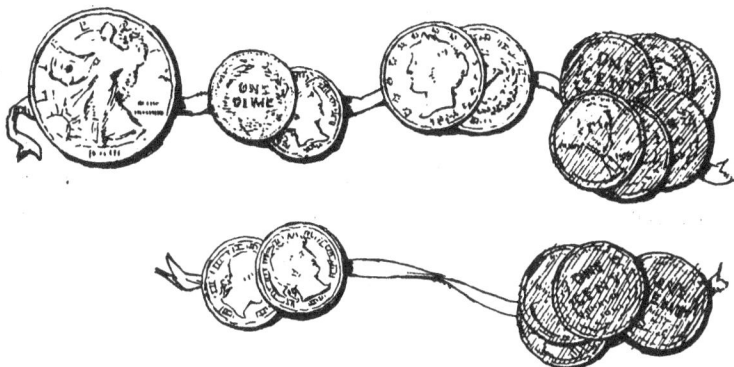

Note: When the lower figure is larger than the upper figure, we borrow 1 from the next column.

1
65
36
—
29

6 from 5 is impossible.  We borrow one from the 6 and place it beside the 5.  This gives us 15.  6 from 15 = 9. In the next column we say 3 from 5, because we borrowed 1 from the 6. 3 from 5 = 2. The difference between 65 and 36 is 29.

80      2 from 10 = 8.
42      4 from  7 = 3.

| Hours | Days | Weeks | Months | Years |
|-------|------|-------|--------|-------|
| 70    | 80   | 90    | 801    | 380   |
| 24    | 42   | 36    | 124    | 126   |

If you buy sugar for 35 cents and meat for 25 cents, how much change would you receive out of 75 cents?

If you had $78.00 in the bank, and paid $59.00 for a wagon, how much would you have left?

How much change should be given in each of the following problems:

| Articles purchased | | Amount paid |
|---|---|---|
| 1 pair of shoes at......$5.75 | | $10.00 |
| 1 knife at ..........1.25 | | 5.00 |
| 1 hat at ...........3.50 | | 10.00 |
| 1 bucket at ..........69 | | 1.00 |
| 8 yards of lace at.....07 | | 5.00 |

### Lesson X

Drill on the following basic subtraction facts:

Subtract:

```
10   11
 5    9
 8    2
 6    8    688   9 from 18 = 9
 7    4    499   9 from 17 = 8
 4    5    189   4 from  5 = 1
 3    3
 2    6    Subtract:
      7    500   6 from 10 = 4
           246   4 from  9 = 5
           254   2 from  4 = 2
```

| 688 | 728 | 917 | 802 | 500 |
|---|---|---|---|---|
| 499 | 509 | 798 | 675 | 246 |

A man earns $19.85 a week.  He puts $2.40 in the bank weekly.  How much does he spend?

Mary had $10.10.  She pays $3.14 for a skirt, $1.85 for a hat.  How much has she left?

Mr. B. earns $125.85 a month and spends $98.67.  How much can he save monthly?

How much change should be given in each of the following problems:

| | | |
|---|---|---|
| 1 suit at ............. | $15.99 | $20.00 |
| 9 spools of thread at .... | .06 | 1.00 |
| 1 pair of gloves at ...... | .97 | 5.00 |
| 7 bars of soap at ........ | .06 | 1.00 |
| Prunes, 35 cts., oranges 10 cts. | | .50 |

### Lesson XI

Teacher's Note: Have pupils read and write miscellaneous numbers to 10,000.

Drill on the following basic subtraction facts:

```
12    13
 9     8      Subtract and test:
 3     7          $87.96
 7     5           13.42
 8     6          $74.54
 6     4           13.42
 5     9          $87.96
 4
```

Subtract:

```
$87.96     $  .80     $80.91     $ 5.00
 13.42        .13      14.46       1.43
-------    -------    -------    -------
$72.31     $80.02     $90.00     $ 5.00
 48.76      14.86      45.75  Prove
```

A woman earns $90.00 a month. She pays $12.35 house rent, $24.62 for groceries and $10.00 other expenses. How much does she save?

A man earns $127.50 a month. He pays $24.50 a month for groceries, $12.00 a month house rent, and $12.18 a month other expenses. How much does he save?

How much change should be given in each of the following problems:

| Articles purchased | Amount paid |
|---|---|
| Sugar, 33 cents; prunes, 27 cents...... | $ 2.00 |
| Raisins, 75 cents; celery, 40 cents........ | 5.00 |
| Oranges, 65 cents; pecans, 53 cents...... | 2.00 |
| Nails, 42 cents; wire, $4.81............ | 10.00 |
| 1 coat at $18.65..................... | 20.00 |

### Lesson XII

Drill on the following subtraction facts:

| 14 | 15 | 16 | 17 | 18 |
|---|---|---|---|---|
| 7 | 7 | 7 | 8 | 9 |
| 6 | 5 | 9 | 9 | |
| 5 | 6 | 8 | | |
| 9 | 9 | | | |
| 8 | | | | |

Subtract and prove:

$100.00      5 from 10 = 5.
  64.85      8 from  9 = 1.
$ 35.15      4 from  9 = 5.
  64.85      6 from  9 = 3.
$100.00

A horse costs $100.00 and a cow $64.85. How much difference between the cost of the horse and the cow?

A house costs $3,110.00 and the lot $857.00. How much difference between the cost of the house and lot?

| $784.95 | $540.60 | $1,000.00 | $75,000.00 |
|---------|---------|-----------|------------|
| 240.35  | 219.25  | 368.37    | 9,865.45   |

| $820.10 | $3,649.00 |
|---------|-----------|
| 274.69  | 1,089.35  |

Prove.

Make an original problem in subtraction.

How much change should be given in each of the following problems:

| Articles purchased | Amount paid |
|--------------------|-------------|
| 1 hat at $3.50 ...................... | $10.00 |
| Sugar, 33 cents; prunes, 27 cents........ | 2.00 |
| 7 bars of soap at 6 cents.............. | 1.00 |
| Oranges, 65 cents; celery, 53 cents...... | 5.00 |

## Lesson XIII

## Multiplication

Type examples in Multiplication:

| 6 | 12 | 14 | 24 | 421 | 156 | 2461 |
|---|----|----|----|-----|-----|------|
| 2 | 3  | 3  | 21 | 26  | 10  | 302  |

Teacher's Note: Dictate miscellaneous numbers to 10,000 and have them read.

Review and write out these tables in home
work books:

| | | | | | | | | | | | |
|---|---|---|---|---|---|---|---|---|---|---|---|
| 2 | 3 | 4 | 5 | $1 \times 2 =$ | 2 | | | | | | 2 |
| 4 | 6 | 8 | 10 | $2 \times 2 =$ | 4 | | | | | 2 | 2 |
| 6 | 9 | 12 | 15 | $3 \times 2 =$ | 6 | | | | 2 | 2 | 2 |
| 8 | 12 | 16 | 20 | $4 \times 2 =$ | 8 | | | 2 | 2 | 2 | 2 |
| 10 | 15 | 20 | 25 | $5 \times 2 =$ | 10 | | 2 | 2 | 2 | 2 | 2 |
| 12 | 18 | 24 | 30 | $6 \times 2 =$ | 12 | | 2 | 2 | 2 | 2 | 2 |
| 14 | 21 | 28 | 35 | $7 \times 2 =$ | 14 | | 4 | 6 | 8 | 10 | 12 |
| 16 | 24 | 32 | 40 | $8 \times 2 =$ | 16 | | $6 \times 2 = 12$ | | | | |
| 18 | 27 | 36 | 45 | $9 \times 2 =$ | 18 | | | | | | |
| 20 | 30 | 40 | 50 | $10 \times 2 =$ | 20 | | | | | | |
| 22 | 33 | 44 | 55 | $11 \times 2 =$ | 22 | | | | | | |
| 24 | 36 | 48 | 60 | $12 \times 2 =$ | 24 | | | | | | |

Note: When the number to be multiplied is
larger than 10, we write the numbers under each
other and multiply each column separately.

Multiply:

14   $2 \times 4 = 8$   Put down the 8 under first
 2   $2 \times 1 = 2$   column.   Put down   the 2
28                  under second column.
                    The product is 28.

Multiply:

| 34 | 23 | 22 |
|---|---|---|
| 2 | 3 | 4 |

Note: When the product in the first column is 10 or more, we set down only the right hand figure and add the other to the product in the second column.  Always begin at the right.

Multiply:

16  $4 \times 6 = 24$  Put down only the 4.  Carry
 4  $4 \times 1 = 4$  the 2 over to the second col-
64          umn. ·Add the 2.  $4 + 2 = 6$.
            The product is 64.

Multiply:

102  $6 \times 2 = 12$  Put down only the 2. Carry
  6  $6 \times 0 = 4$   the 1 over to the second col-
612  $6 \times 1 = 6$   umn.   Add  the  1.    Put
            down the 6.

Multiply:

| 23 | 39 | 25 | 14 | 480 | 207 |
|----|----|----|----|-----|-----|
| 4  | 2  | 3  | 7  | 2   | 4   |

Find the number of cabbages in 3 rows if there are 131 in each row?

How far can you ride in 6 hours on a train that goes at the rate of 43 miles an hour?

A flour barrel holds 196 pounds of flour. How many pounds will 5 barrels hold?

Problem in subtraction for review: Columbus discovered America in 1492.  How many years have passed since then?

**Lesson XIV**

Multiplication

| 6  | 7  |
|----|----|
| 12 | 14 |
| 18 | 21 |
| 24 | 28 |
| 30 | 35 |
| 36 | 42 |
| 42 | 49 |
| 48 | 56 |
| 54 | 63 |
| 60 | 70 |
| 66 | 77 |
| 72 | 84 |

Write these tables out in full in home work notebook:

$1 \times 6 = 6$
$2 \times 6 = 12$, etc.

Note: When both numbers are 10 or more, we multiply by each figure in the lower numbers separately and add the two products.

Multiply:

```
 13
 12
 26
 13
156
```

When we multiply by the 1 in the 12, we must be careful to put the first figure in the column under the 1. This means that the 3 comes under the 2 and not under the 6.

Multiply:

| 24 | 23 | 32 | 132 | 225 | 462 |
|----|----|----|-----|-----|-----|
| 12 | 24 | 23 | 11  | 43  | 30  |

How many crates of strawberries are on a train of 20 cars, each of which contains 725 crates?

Multiply:

```
      780          or            780
      304                        304
     ————                       ————
     3120                       3120
      000                      2340
     2340                     ——————
   ———————                    237120
    237120
```

Multiply:

```
  308      340      307      780
   32       24       43      304
  ————     ————     ————     ————
```

Find the cost of 809 tickets at 75 cents each.

Make out receipt to Mr. James N. Thornton for payment of $25.35.

### Lesson XV
### Multiplication

Read and write miscellaneous numbers to 100,000.

```
 8      Write the 8 table out in full in home
16      work notebooks:
24
32          1 × 8 = 8
40          2 × 8 = 16, etc.
48
56      Multiply:
64              160
72               15
80             ————
88              800
96              160
               ————
               2400
```

If it costs 15 cents per day for a child's education, what does it cost per year of 160 days?

If it costs 15 cents per school day to pay for one child's education, how much of the tax-payers' money is lost when a child loses 57 days of the term?

There are 2383 children of Buncombe County enrolled in the first grade and 802 enrolled in the seventh. How many more in the first than in the seventh? How is it in your County? Why is it so?

Not long ago the average salary paid teachers in the county schools of North Carolina was $91.33. In 1934 it is about $60.00. What is the decrease in salary? To get good teachers for our children, we must pay good salaries.

Make out bill to Mrs. James W. Thornton for the following items:

4 doz. eggs @ . .$ .40
12 hens @ . . . . . . 1.00
15 friers @ . . . . .50
4 doz. corn @ . . .50
3 pks. peaches . . .75

### Lesson XVI

Multiplication

| 9 | 63 |
| 18 | 72 |
| 27 | 81 |
| 36 | 90 |
| 45 | 99 |
| 54 | 108 |

Write out this table in full in home work notebooks:

Multiply:

```
   344            6007
   600              42
 206400          12014
                 24028
                252294
```

Multiply:

| 4325 | 4806 | 5473 |
|------|------|------|
| 6    | 8    | 23   |

If you can save $3.85 a week, how much can you save in a month?

A man pays $45.55 monthly rent for his country store and 7 times as much for a large city building. How much is his city rent?

Driving a car 896 miles a month, how many miles will you drive it a year? 18 months? 3 years?

By putting $1.75 a week in building and loan, how much can you save a year? In 6 years? 6½ years?

It costs $3,578.00 to build a house and 37 times as much to build a hotel. How much does the hotel cost?

### Lesson XVII

### Multiplication

Write out 6 tables in full in home work notebooks and drill in class.

Make Roman numbers from I to XX.

| I   | VI   | XI    | XVI   |
|-----|------|-------|-------|
| II  | VII  | XII   | XVII  |
| III | VIII | XIII  | XVIII |
| IV  | IX   | XIV   | XIX   |
| V   | X    | XV    | XX    |

$$I = 1 \qquad\qquad X = 10$$
$$II = 1 + 1 \qquad\qquad IX = 10 - 1 = 9$$
$$V = 5 \qquad\qquad XI = 10 + 1$$
$$IV = 5 - 1 = 4 \qquad XIX = 10 + 9$$
$$VI = 5 + 1 = 6 \qquad XX = 10 + 10$$

Find cost of:

| | |
|---|---|
| 7 doz. eggs @ . . . . . . . . | $    .45 |
| 4 pounds of coffee @ . . . . | .35 |
| 6 yards of silk @ . . . . . . | 2.75 |
| 8 bags of flour @ . . . . . . | 1.25 |
| 25 acres of land @ . . . . . . | 135.00 |

I bought 8 yards of gingham at 12½ cents a yard. What change should I get back from a $5.00 bill?

Pupils work any 4 multiplication problems previously worked in class.

Make one original problem in multiplication.

### Lesson XVIII
Multiplication

Write out in full 7 and 8 tables and drill on them.

Make Roman numbers from XX to L (20 to 50).

| | |
|---|---|
| XXI | XXVI |
| XXII | XXVII |
| XXIII | XXVIII |
| XXIV | XXIX |
| XXV | XXX |

$$XXX = 10 + 10 + 10 = 30$$
$$L = 50$$
$$XL = 50 - 10 = 40$$

Multiply:

| 6507 | 7348 | 7564 |
|------|------|------|
| 346 | 506 | 308 |

At $0.35 a dozen, how much will you pay for 5 doz. eggs?

A woman earns $4.50 a day. How much will she earn in 30 days?

### Lesson XIX

Multiplication

Write out in full the 9 table and drill on it.

Make Roman numbers from L to C. (50 to 100).

$$L = 50$$
$$LX = 50 + 10 = 60$$
$$LXX = 50 + 10 + 10 = 70$$
$$LXXX = 80$$
$$C = 100$$
$$XC = 100 - 10 = 90$$

Multiply:

| 6408 | $526.34 | $92.74 |
|------|---------|--------|
| 49 | 123 | 785 |

If a woman pays $12.75 a month for house rent, how much will she pay a year?

A man paid $0.80 a bushel for 15 bushels of corn, $1.25 a bushel for 12 bushels of wheat and $0.75 a bushel for 8 bushels of rye. How much did he pay in all?

## Lesson XX

The Farmers' Federation bought 384 coops of chickens, each coop containing 96 pounds. How many pounds did they buy?

At 23 cents a pound, how much did these chickens cost?

Pupils work 2 review problems in addition, subtraction, multiplication, and division.

Read the following sentence:

There were 122,775,046 people in the United States when the 1930 census was taken.

# Arithmetic
# Second Twenty Lessons

### Lesson I

## Division

Teacher's Note: Some of the examples in each lesson are to be worked at home and some in class. In teaching a new process, the teacher will find it helpful to have pupil work examples in class, erase the answers and work same examples at home by himself before the next lesson.

Type examples in division:

$3\overline{)6933}$

$3\overline{)1269}$

2
2
2
2
2
2
—
12

$12 \div 2 = 6$

$2\overline{)12}$
6

$2\overline{)40}$
20

2 goes into 4 twice, 2 will not go into 0. There are 20 twos in 40.

Note: Sometimes when we divide, there is something left over:

$13\frac{1}{2}$
2)27

2 goes into 2, once.
2 goes into 7, 3 times and 1 left over.

253
2)506

2 goes into 5, twice and 1 left over. We put the 1 beside the 0 and say, 2 goes into 10, 5 times. 2 goes into 6, 3 times. $506 \div 2 = 253$.

147
3)441

To prove: multiply $147 \times 3$.

    147
      3
    441

Teach division sign:

2)424  2)248  3)366          3)724  4)848  2)910

                                4)5208  5)5065

Teacher's Note: The teacher may make above problems concrete by using local terms: boxes of oranges, bushels of wheat, pounds of ice, etc.

How many knives at $2.00 can be bought for $140.00?

A dealer has 164 tires. How many cars can he equip with 4 tires each?

## Lesson II

### Division

Find the cost of:

1 dozen eggs if 4 dozen cost................$ 1.40
1 can of corn if 5 cans cost...............     .75

1 pound of coffee if 3 pounds cost........$  1.05
1 bag of flour if 8 bags cost.............  10.00
1 acre of land if 5 acres cost............ 675.00

How many weeks in 63 days?  In 3,045 days?
If you can earn $21.00 a week, how much will you
earn in 42 days?

Teacher's Note: The teacher may make the following problems concrete
by use of local terms.

$$\begin{array}{ll} 2252 \\ 4)\overline{9008} \end{array} \qquad \begin{array}{r} 2252 \\ 4 \\ \hline 9008 \end{array} \qquad \begin{array}{l} 321\frac{2}{8} \\ 8)\overline{2570} \end{array} \qquad \text{Prove:} \qquad \begin{array}{r} 321 \\ 8 \\ \hline 2568 \\ 2 \\ \hline 2570 \end{array}$$

Divide and prove:

$9)\overline{1989}$    $8)\overline{2568}$    $7)\overline{2247}$    $6)\overline{3258}$

$5)\overline{3210}$    $4)\overline{1856}$    $3)\overline{2586}$    $2)\overline{1332}$

## Lesson III

### Division

Divide and prove:

$9)\overline{1989}$   $8)\overline{2568}$   $6)\overline{3258}$   $5)\overline{3210}$   $4)\overline{1856}$

$3)\overline{2586}$   $5)\overline{3210}$   $4)\overline{1856}$   $3)\overline{2500}$   $2)\overline{1302}$

$9)\overline{7488}$   $8)\overline{4256}$   $7)\overline{2007}$   $6)\overline{3258}$   $2)\overline{1332}$

If a man raises 210 bushels of corn on 7 acres of
land, how much is that per acre?  How much can he
raise on 25 acres?

Each pupil make one or more problems in division from his own experience.

## Lesson IV

### Division

Divide and prove:

9)7227        8)2432        7)3563        6)4036

5)2035        4)3616        3)2718        2)1800

How many sweaters at $7.00 each can be bought for $32,613.00?

Copy or write from dictation numbers to 1,000,000.

## Lesson V

### Division

Divide and prove:

9)3890        8)3450        2)1059        7)3775

6)19001       5)3242        4)5323        3)2875

Teacher's Note: Teacher may make these examples concrete by using local terms: bales of cotton, pounds of tobacco, bushels of corn, etc.

If 9 acres of land cost $3,285.00, find cost of 1 acre.

How many weeks in 5,278 days?

How many yards in 8,736 feet?

How many gallons in 3,368 quarts?

Each pupil make one original problem in division taken from his own experience.

## Lesson VI

Division

Review all examples in short division. Make three original problems in class.

Teacher's Note: Teacher may make following examples concrete by use of local terms.

Short division:                     Long division:

$$
\begin{array}{r}
286 \\
3\overline{)858}
\end{array}
$$

$$
\begin{array}{r}
286 \\
3\overline{)858} \\
6 \\
\overline{25} \\
24 \\
\overline{18} \\
18 \\
\overline{\phantom{0}}
\end{array}
$$

Teacher's Note: a. For divisors use  20, 30, 40, 50, etc.
                                       21, 31, 41, 51, etc.
                                       29, 39, 49, 59, etc.
Then any intervening numbers
    b. Types to avoid:      42$\overline{)4284}$     29$\overline{)1152}$     18$\overline{)1004}$

Type examples in Long Division:

$$
\begin{array}{r}
347 \\
11\overline{)3817} \\
33 \\
\overline{51} \\
44 \\
\overline{77} \\
77 \\
\overline{\phantom{0}}
\end{array}
$$

11 into 38 = 3. 3 × 11 = 33. The remainder is 5. We bring down the 1 beside the 5 and have 51. 11 into 51 = 4. 4 × 11 = 44. The remainder is 7. We bring down the 7 and have 77. The answer is 347.

$$
\begin{array}{r}
347 \\
11 \\
\overline{347} \\
347 \\
\overline{3817}
\end{array}
$$

Divide and prove:

11)3564    11)9075    21)1071    51)5661    31)1147

## Lesson VII

Division

```
      104
32)3328              104
   32                 32
  ───                ───
   128               208
   128               312
   ───              ────
                    3328
```

Divide and prove:

11)21004        11)70088        11)35055

41)9922         31)1488         51)4284


A man sold 11 bushels of potatoes for $9.35.  How much did he get per bushel?  How much would he get for 85 bushels?

There are 32 pounds in 1 bushel of oats.  How many bushels in 21,184 pounds of oats?

Make Roman numbers to XX.

Take from dictation and add:

```
$    345.85
     23.47
       .85
     10.00
       .50
       .05
  8,325.75
  ────────
```

## Lesson VIII

### Division

$$143\tfrac{21}{60}$$
$$60\overline{)8601}$$
$$\underline{60}$$
$$260$$
$$\underline{240}$$
$$201$$
$$\underline{180}$$
$$21$$

$$45\tfrac{4}{8}$$
$$8\overline{)364}$$

Divide:

$$72\overline{)4686} \qquad 42\overline{)1558} \qquad 93\overline{)3094} \qquad 53\overline{)3900}$$

If 21 tons of coal cost $157.50, find cost of 1 ton.

Divide half a dozen numbers by 100.

If a man earns $1,000.00 in 10 months, how much will he earn a month?

A man raises 4,300 bushels of corn on 100 acres. How much will he raise on 1 acre?

Mrs. Miles sold 560 pounds of shelled corn for $84.00. How much did she get per pound?

## Lesson IX

### Division

$$104\tfrac{83}{86}$$
$$86\overline{)9027}$$
$$\underline{86}$$
$$427$$
$$\underline{344}$$
$$83$$

Divide and prove:

24)9086        74)4608        34)1536

40)2856        82)9020        44)1134

How many months in 286,160 days?

How many years in 912 months?

How many feet in 4,092 inches?

The Farmers Federation spent $56.00 for automobile tires at $14.00 per tire. How many tires did they buy?

## Lesson X

### Division

Divide and prove:

33)1419        64)7040        44)3476

34)2070        56)3472        68)7353

If a train travels 52 miles an hour, how long will it take to travel 2,444 miles?

If you travel 150 miles on 10 gallons of gas, how much mileage to the gallon?

Mr. Gray left an estate of 40,505 acres of valuable land to be divided among 54 people. What was the share of each?

The Farmers Federation bought 384 coops of chickens, each coop containing 96 pounds. How many pounds did they buy? How much did these chickens cost at 23 cents a pound?

## Lesson XI

### Division

```
            858
407)349206
    3256
    2360
    2035
    3256
    3256
```

Teacher's Note: Teacher may make the following examples concrete by using terms of local interests and occupations:

## Divide and prove:

```
59)4248        88)7656        78)2730
```

```
604)472932         503)234901
```

Mr. Moss earns $4.95 a day.  How many days will it take him to earn $1,024.65?

Mr. James pays 49 men $314.09.  How much is in each man's pay envelope if they earn equal amounts?

## Lesson XII

### Division

Teacher's Note: Teacher may make the following examples concrete by using terms of local interests and occupations: products of cotton mills, of furniture plants, of tobacco sales, etc.

## Divide and prove:

```
328)615,008        225)14,850        535)353,010
```

```
224)970,536
```

How many years are there in 286,160 days?

Mr. Jenkins earns $2,800.00 a year.  How much does he earn a month?  A week?  A day?

## Lesson XIII

### Division

Make out a bill and receipt.

Divide 46,807 by 31; by 56; by 79; by 274; by 305.

How many feet are there in 2,520 inches?

A grocer bought 34 crates of strawberries for $63.80. Find the price per crate.

The Woolworth Building in New York is 792 feet high. How many times as high is it as a house 35 feet high?

If a man has 1,080 tomatoes to pack in boxes of 45 each, how many boxes will he need?

The ages of the pupils in a night school class are 28, 19, 34, 21, 40, 35. Find the average age.

Pupil make original problem in division from his own experience.

If a fruit dealer paid $920.75 for 456 boxes of apples, how much did he pay for a box?

## Lesson XIV

### Fractions

Into what parts is a foot ruler divided?

Name all divisions on a yard stick.

How many halves in a whole apple?

How many quarters in a whole apple?

How many $\frac{1}{16}$ths in a whole apple?

How many whole apples in $\frac{2}{2}$ of an apple?

How many whole apples in $\frac{6}{2}$ apples?

How many whole dollars in $\frac{9}{3}$ dollars?

Divide this line into halves, then quarters, then eighths————————————

Divide this line into thirds, into sixths, into twelfths————————————————————

Type examples in fractions:

$$\frac{1}{4} + \frac{1}{4}$$

$$\frac{1}{4} + \frac{2}{4}$$

$$\frac{1}{3} + \frac{1}{6}$$

$$\frac{2}{3} + \frac{5}{6}$$

$$\frac{2}{3} + \frac{5}{6} + \frac{2}{3}$$

Add:

$$\frac{2}{3}$$
$$\frac{1}{3}$$
$$\overline{\frac{3}{3}}$$    $\frac{2}{3} + \frac{1}{3} = \frac{3}{3} = 1.$

$$\frac{3}{4}$$
$$\frac{3}{4}$$
$$\overline{\frac{6}{4}}$$    $\frac{3}{4} + \frac{3}{4} = \frac{6}{4} = 1\frac{2}{4}.$

$$2\frac{1}{3}$$
$$1\frac{1}{3}$$
$$3\frac{1}{3}$$
$$\overline{6\frac{3}{3}} = 7$$

Add:

| $\frac{5}{8}$ | $\frac{5}{7}$ | $6\frac{2}{3}$ |
| $\frac{3}{8}$ | $\frac{3}{7}$ | $4\frac{2}{3}$ |

| $2\frac{1}{3}$ | $4\frac{1}{3}$ | $5\frac{2}{3}$ |
| $1\frac{1}{3}$ | $3$ | $\frac{1}{3}$ |
| $3\frac{1}{3}$ | $1\frac{1}{3}$ | $3\frac{1}{3}$ |

If it takes $2\frac{1}{2}$ yards of cloth for a blouse and $3\frac{1}{2}$ for a skirt; how many yards are needed for both?

What is the sum of $3\frac{1}{4}$ miles, $4\frac{3}{4}$ miles and $\frac{1}{4}$ mile?

The following recipe makes enough baked custard to serve 8 people:

$$2 \text{ cups scalded milk}$$
$$4 \text{ eggs}$$
$$\tfrac{1}{4} \text{ cup of sugar}$$
$$\tfrac{1}{8} \text{ teaspoon of salt}$$
$$\tfrac{1}{2} \text{ teaspoon of vanilla}$$

Change this to make enough to serve 16 **people;** 4 people.

## Lesson XV

### Fractions

Add:

$$23\tfrac{1}{4} = 23\tfrac{1}{4} \qquad\qquad 52\tfrac{5}{6} = 52\tfrac{5}{6}$$
$$15\tfrac{1}{4} = 15\tfrac{1}{4} \qquad\qquad 34\tfrac{1}{3} = 34\tfrac{2}{6}$$
$$45\tfrac{1}{2} = 45\tfrac{2}{4} \qquad\qquad \overline{86\tfrac{7}{6}} = 87\tfrac{1}{6}$$
$$\overline{83\tfrac{4}{4}} = 84$$

Add:

$$52\tfrac{5}{6} \qquad\qquad 36\tfrac{1}{2} \qquad\qquad 63\tfrac{1}{3}$$
$$\underline{28\tfrac{1}{2}} \qquad\qquad \underline{14\tfrac{1}{6}} \qquad\qquad \underline{25\tfrac{1}{6}}$$

$$14\tfrac{1}{2} \quad 31\tfrac{5}{6} \quad 42\tfrac{2}{3} \quad 27\tfrac{1}{3} \quad 64\tfrac{1}{6}$$
$$25\tfrac{1}{6} \quad 9\tfrac{1}{3} \quad 6\tfrac{1}{6} \quad 12\tfrac{1}{6} \quad 5\tfrac{1}{2}$$
$$\underline{46\tfrac{1}{2}} \quad \underline{24\tfrac{1}{6}} \quad \underline{37\tfrac{1}{3}} \quad \underline{42\tfrac{1}{6}} \quad \underline{13\tfrac{5}{6}}$$

Mabel picked $4\tfrac{1}{3}$ dozen violets and $1\tfrac{5}{6}$ dozen tulips. How many dozen flowers did she pick?

Pupil make problem from his own experience in addition of fractions.

## Lesson XVI

### Fractions

Teacher's Note: Give drill in finding common denominators by inspection.

Add:
$$7\tfrac{1}{3} = 7\tfrac{4}{12}$$
$$8\tfrac{1}{2} = 8\tfrac{6}{12}$$
$$7\tfrac{3}{4} = 7\tfrac{9}{12}$$
$$22\tfrac{19}{12} = 23\tfrac{7}{12}$$

Subtract:
$$36\tfrac{1}{2} = 36\tfrac{3}{6}$$
$$14\tfrac{1}{6} = 14\tfrac{1}{6}$$
$$22\tfrac{2}{6}$$

If a man works $7\tfrac{1}{3}$ hours one day, $8\tfrac{1}{2}$ hours the second day and $7\tfrac{3}{4}$ hours the third day; how many hours will he work in the three days?

Make problems concrete with local terms:

Subtract:

| $44\tfrac{1}{2}$ | $82\tfrac{3}{4}$ | $61\tfrac{1}{2}$ | $72\tfrac{1}{2}$ |
|---|---|---|---|
| $36\tfrac{1}{2}$ | $42\tfrac{1}{4}$ | $42\tfrac{1}{2}$ | $31\tfrac{1}{2}$ |

| $36\tfrac{1}{2}$ | $52\tfrac{5}{6}$ | $66\tfrac{1}{3}$ | $38\tfrac{2}{3}$ |
|---|---|---|---|
| $14\tfrac{1}{6}$ | $34\tfrac{1}{3}$ | $25\tfrac{1}{6}$ | $19\tfrac{1}{6}$ |

From a bunch of bananas containing $8\tfrac{5}{6}$ dozen, a dealer sold $2\tfrac{1}{2}$ dozen; how many dozen had he left?

A wagon with a load weighs $2\tfrac{1}{4}$ tons. The wagon alone weighs $\tfrac{3}{5}$ of a ton. What is the weight of the load?

## Lesson XVII

### Fractions

Multiply:

$\frac{3}{4} \times \frac{5}{7} = \frac{15}{28}$

$32 \times \frac{3}{4} = \frac{96}{4} = 24$

$$
\begin{array}{r}
27 \\
2\frac{2}{3} \\
\hline
18 \\
54 \\
\hline
72
\end{array}
$$

$\frac{1}{3}$ of $27 = \phantom{0}9$

$\frac{2}{3}$ of $27 = 18$

$2 \times 27 = 54$

$54 + 18 = 72$

Note: Teacher may make the following examples concrete by using terms of local interests and occupations.

Multiply:  $168 \times \frac{2}{3}$;    $145 \times \frac{2}{5}$;    $224 \times \frac{3}{4}$.

Mr. Baird's salary is $984.00 and his expenses are $\frac{3}{4}$ of this amount; how much are his yearly expenses?

How much should a plumber get for $6\frac{1}{2}$ hours work at 95 cents an hour?

A farmer has 64 acres of wheat, yielding $24\frac{1}{2}$ bushels per acre; what will it cost him for threshing at $6\frac{1}{2}$ cents a bushel?   If he sells his crop at $132\frac{1}{2}$ per bushel, how much will he have left, after paying the thresher's bill?

## Lesson XVIII

### Fractions

Find the cost of: $7\frac{3}{4}$ yards of cloth at 72 cents; $8\frac{2}{3}$ yards of carpet at $1.08; $15\frac{3}{8}$ gallons of gasoline at 24 cents; $25\frac{5}{6}$ dozen ears of corn at 18 cents.

Note: Teacher may make the following examples concrete by using local terms.

Multiply:     $37 \times 17\frac{3}{4}$;          $46 \times 25\frac{2}{3}$;
              $54 \times 42\frac{3}{5}$;          $79 \times 38\frac{1}{6}$.

Find the value of 5 beef cattle weighing respectively 950 pounds, 860 pounds, 795 pounds, 900 pounds and 896 pounds at $9\frac{3}{4}$ cents per pound.

A meadow of 96 acres averaged $1\frac{4}{5}$ tons of hay per acre; what was the total production?

If it required $1\frac{3}{4}$ bushels of seed wheat to sow one acre, how many bushels are needed to sow 26 acres?

$$6 \div \tfrac{1}{3} = 6 \times \tfrac{3}{1} = 18$$
$$\tfrac{3}{6} \div \tfrac{5}{8} = \tfrac{3}{6} \times \tfrac{8}{5} = \tfrac{24}{30} = \tfrac{4}{5}$$
$$8\tfrac{1}{2} \div 3\tfrac{2}{3}$$
$$8\tfrac{1}{2} = \tfrac{17}{2}$$
$$3\tfrac{2}{3} = \tfrac{11}{3}$$
$$\tfrac{17}{2} \div \tfrac{11}{3} = \tfrac{17}{2} \times \tfrac{3}{11} = \tfrac{51}{22} = 2\tfrac{7}{22}$$

Divide:

6 by $\tfrac{1}{3}$; $\tfrac{3}{6}$ by $\tfrac{5}{8}$; $15\tfrac{2}{3}$ by $4\tfrac{5}{6}$; 7 by $3\tfrac{3}{4}$; $\tfrac{5}{8}$ by $\tfrac{3}{4}$; $6\tfrac{3}{4}$ by $5\tfrac{1}{3}$; $8\tfrac{1}{2}$ by $3\tfrac{2}{3}$; $\tfrac{5}{12}$ by $\tfrac{7}{8}$; $20\tfrac{1}{4}$ by $14\tfrac{1}{3}$.

How many towels can be made from a strip of linen $12\frac{3}{5}$ yards long, if $\tfrac{4}{5}$ of a yard is required for one towel?

How many yards of cloth at $33\frac{1}{3}$ cents can be bought for $18.00?

## Lesson XIX

$ 400.00
.04
───────
$16.0000    Interest for 1 year at 4%.
4
───────
$64.00    Interest for 4 years at 4%.

Find the interest at 4% on:

$400.00 for 1 year; for 4 years.

$800.00 for 5 years and 6 months.

$ 36.24 for $4\frac{1}{2}$ years.

$ 28.65 for 8 months, 8 years, and for 4 months at 6%.

$ 98.30 for 3 years and 9 months.

Pupil make 1 problem from his own experience.

## Lesson XX

Have test on problems most needed by pupils.

Find interest on $350.80 from 1st of January, 1905, to the 1st of November, 1906.

Find interest on $540.96 from the 9th of April, 1904, to the 9th of March, 1906.

Find interest on $1,500.00 from the 7th of September, 1920, to the 31st of December, 1924.

# Phonics

Teachers note: Experience has shown that good results are secured by first acquainting pupils with sounds of consonants, vowels and blends, and teaching a few phonograms and how to puzzle out a few new words, then covering practically the same ground again with more intensive drill. It is suggested, therefore, that these twenty lessons serve as the basis of a second twenty-lesson course, special stress being laid on those points most needed by the class.

With some classes it may be advisable to give only part of the lesson indicated, taking up the remainder in succeeding lessons. In that case, this outline may be expanded into a forty lesson course.

Better results are obtained when the drill in phonics is given in a separate period from the reading lesson.

With Reading, **Lesson, I** no phonics.

## Lesson II, with Reading

TEACHER: I am going to write a word on the board. (Writes "like.") I hope you will "like" it. Would you "like" to know what it is?

PUPIL: It is "like." It was in our lesson five times to-day.

TEACHER: I "l-ike" that answer. Now, will you "l-isten" while I say "l-ike" and "l-esson" and "l-et" and "l-etter"? Don't all of them sound alike at the beginning—l-isten, l-ike, l-esson, l-et, l-etter? I'm going to write the letter that has this sound. (Writes "l.") It is "l." There are two of you whose names begin with this same sound. Can you guess whose names they are?

PUPIL: My name is Lena. Isn't that one?

SECOND PUPIL: And mine is Lester and it starts that way.

TEACHER: Good. I was thinking of L-ena and L-ester. I shall write a capital "L" now for names begin with capitals, don't they? (Writes "L.") L-ena, since "L" is your letter, will you tell me some of the words that I used that begin with "l"?

LENA: I remember "l-ike" and "l-esson."

TEACHER: Good. "L-ike" was in your "l-esson," so I'm especially glad you remembered those two. Now, Lester, can you tell us the others?

LESTER: I remember "l-et" and "l-etter."

TEACHER: Good. That is all of them except "l-isten" (sounds). Can any one say all five of the l-words and the two L-names?

PUPIL: l-ike, l-esson, l-et, l-etter, l-isten, L-ena, L-ester.

### Follow Up Work
Write *l l l l l*

## Lesson III

Teacher: Can any one tell me why we talked about "L-ena's" and "L-ester's" names in our "l-ast lesson"?

Pupil: We talked about their names because they began with "L" (sounds). And I've been thinking that we ought to have talked about my last name, too, because it is "L-awrence."

Teacher: Why, surely, Mr. L-awrence, you have an L-name, too (sounds). I should have thought of that, but I'm glad that you thought of it first. Now, we have three L-names; will some one give me three other l-words?

Pupil: l-ike, l-esson, l-et, l-etter.

Teacher: Fine, one more than I asked for! Mr. Lawrence, will you give me the three L-names and five l-words?

Mr. Lawrence: l-ike, l-esson, l-isten, l-et, l-etter, L-ena, L-ester, L-awrence.

Teacher: Perfect, Mr. L-awrence. Now, I want to tell you two stories that I l-earned about "l" (sounds) and see which you think is the better story. One teacher told me that "l" sounded like a cracked cow bell—l-l-l——and another teacher said it was like the sound made by telegraph wires—l-l-l. Of which does it remind you?

Pupil: I've pressed my ear close to a telegraph pole many a time to listen to the noise of the wires, and I think it does remind me of that—l-l-l.

Teacher: All right, then, we will choose the telegraph wire sound—l-l-l. In our l-esson to-day, we had another "l" word. Do you know what it was?

Pupil: (No answer).

Teacher: Suppose we "l-ook" and see if we can find it. "L-isten" while I read the second sentence: "Do you l-ove your home?"

Several Pupils: "L-ove"!

Teacher: Exactly! Now, we have l-ike and l-ove in our "l" collection. And since I've been talking to you to-day, I've used two others. I said that I had "l-earned" two stories about "l."

Pupil: "L-earned"!

Teacher: Good. Just now I said, "Suppose we 'l-ook' and see." L-ena, what is our "l" word there?

Lena: "L-ook," isn't it?

Teacher: Yes. So now we have two more "l" words, "l-earn" and "l-ook." If we l-ike and l-ove and l-ook and l-isten we can l-earn the l-essons of l-ife, can't we?

### Follow Up Work

Write *lllll   LLLLL*

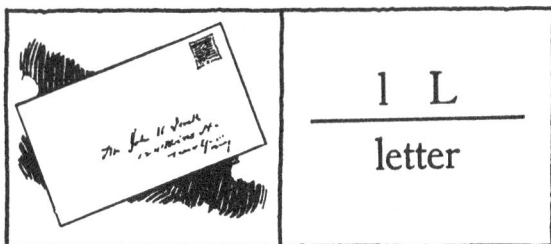

1  L
letter

## Lesson IV

TEACHER: We had two l-words in our l-esson to-day. Does any one remember them? L-et's l-ook for them. L-isten while L-ester reads the first sentence.

LESTER: I l-ove my mother and my father.

PUPILS: "L-ove," of course.

TEACHER: Lena, will you read the last sentence?

LENA: My mother and my father l-ike my home.

PUPILS: Why, it's "l-ike," the very first of our l-words!

TEACHER: Good. Now, while you are l-ooking at the l-esson, I want to tell you the story of another l-etter. These stories of what the letters sound l-ike always amuse me but they do help me remember the sounds. There is only one story for this letter and I believe you can guess the story as soon as I sound the letter. The letter that I'm thinking of sounds like this—m-m-m. Doesn't that remind you of something?

SEVERAL PUPILS: It sounds like a cow mooing.

TEACHER: Good. That is what I had in "m-ind." (Writes "m" on the board.) This letter is "m" and is easy to sound— m-m-m. While I read the first sentence in the lesson, will you listen for the "m" sound? (Reads) I love "m-y" "m-other" and "m-y" father.

PUPIL: "m-y" has that sound.

SECOND PUPIL: And "m-other" begins that way, too.

THIRD PUPIL: And there's another "m-y."

TEACHER: Good. In the second sentence, how m-any "m's" do you hear? (Reads) I love "m-y" sister and "m-y" brother.

PUPIL: The two "m-y's" begin with that sound.

TEACHER: Good! Now, listen for "m's" (sounds) in the next sentence. (Reads) "M-y" "m-other" and "m-y" father love "m-e."

PUPIL: Two "m-y's," "m-other," and "m-e."

TEACHER: Good enough! So we have three "m" words in the lesson—"m-y," "m-other," "m-e," and I've used two others in talking with you. "M-ind" and "m-any." You used one when you spoke of the "m-ooing" of the cow. Can any one give three or four of these "m" words?

PUPIL: "m-y," "m-other," "m-e," "m-oo," and "m-y" name is "M-ary."

TEACHER: Hurrah for you, M-ary, for claiming your letter! (Writes capital "M" on board.) Does any one remember the two "m" words that I used in talking?

PUPILS: (No answer.)

TEACHER: "M-ind" and "m-any." I said I had something in m-ind and I asked how m-any "m's" were in the sentence. Suppose we put our "m" words together in a sentence to help us keep them in m-ind—"M-y m-other told M-ary m-any times to m-ind m-e."

### Follow Up Work

Write *m, m, m, m    M, M, M, M*

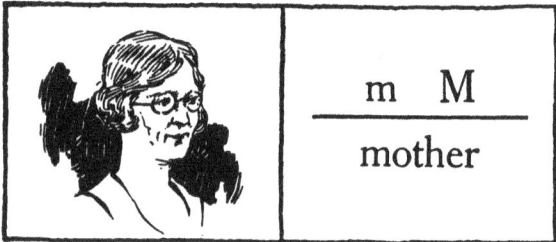

m    M

mother

## Lesson V

TEACHER: Turn to the lesson that we read tonight. It has only one l-word, but you will find it six times.

RESPONSIVE PUPIL: It is l-ike, l-ike, l-ike, l-ike, l-ike, l-ike!

TEACHER: Good! Suppose we say it together, class, six times, holding on to the "l" a little longer than usual.

TEACHER AND CLASS: L-ike, l-ike, l-ike, l-ike, l-ike, l-ike.

TEACHER: I used two new l-words just now. Did any one notice them?

PUPILS: (No answer).

TEACHER: I asked you to hold on to "l" a l-ittle l-onger than usual.

SEVERAL PUPILS: l-ittle and l-onger.

ONE PUPIL: I don't know why I didn't spot those words at first, because I've been watching out for "l" and "m" words when people are talking. This morning my mother said, "I must give you some milk for lunch." She laughed when I said it after her this way: "I m-ust give you some m-ilk for l-unch." But I told her I had to gather up "l" and "m" words for Night School. So I've brought you "m-ust" and "m-ilk" and "l-unch."

TEACHER: That's just the way to go at it, Mr. Jenkins. You will soon be able to "spot" new words in your reading lesson that same way. Now, please let me see your l-cards. (Cards are passed forward.) These are fine! What is our key word for "l"?

MANY PUPILS: L-etter!

TEACHER: Good! Now I'm going to begin the key sentence for "l" and see how many can complete it: "If we l-ike and l-ove and "l—"

LENA: "If we l-ike and l-ove and l-ook and l-isten we can l-earn the l-essons of l-ife."

TEACHER: Good for you, Lena. Let's say it all together, class.

TEACHER AND CLASS: "If we l-ike and l-ove and l-ook and l-isten we can l-earn the l-essons of l-ife."

TEACHER: Mr. Jenkins gave us a start on our other letter with his "m-ust" and "m-ilk." Who will give me some of our other m-words?

PUPIL: M-other, m-e, m-y.

TEACHER: Good! Please give me your m-cards. (Cards are passed forward.) I am proud of these. I see that some of you found pictures of "m-other" and pasted them on instead of drawing them, and some have drawn very good pictures indeed. How many remember the m-sentence we made about m-other and M-ary?

MARY: "M-y m-other told M-ary m-any times to m-ind m-e."

TEACHER: M-ary has given us the m-sentence and L-ena gave us the l-sentence. I'm glad they were the first ones to learn their own sentences. I hope they will each drill three or four of their friends on their sentences, so that soon all of us can think of them right away. A little later on, when we are doing more writing, we shall make a chart of all of our key sentences.

MR. JENKINS: You gave us one more l-word then. You said "l-ater."

ANOTHER PUPIL: And I spotted two m-words, too. You said "m-ake" and "m-ore."

TEACHER: Good work, Mr. Jenkins and Mr. Hawkins. You are certainly on the job. Now, there is another letter for us to learn tonight. It is easy to sound and I shall never forget how funny I thought it was when my teacher first taught it to me. She growled just like a dog that had had his bone taken away from him, "r-r-r," and then wrote "r" on the board. (Writes "r" on board.) Some of us caught the spirit so well that we couldn't keep from shaking our heads when we growled "r-r-r." But, at any rate, I've never forgotten it and it is the only growling thing that I like.

PUPIL: Well, I'm glad you do like it because I'll have to claim it for mine, because my name is, Ragan Reed.

TEACHER: Why, Mr. Reed, it seems to be yours twice, once for Ragan and once for Reed. (Writes capital "R" on board.) So whenever you want to growl, it will be all right with us. (Laughter.) Now, for some other "r" words.

PUPIL: In our lesson to-day, we had "r-ead" and I thought of "r-est."

SECOND PUPIL: "R-un" and "r-ock" are good r-words, aren't they?

TEACHER: Very good r-words indeed, and now we have enough for our key sentences: "R-un to the r-ock and r-est and r-ead." Mr. R-agan R-eed, we shall turn that key sentence over to you and our key word for our card will be "r-ock."

### Follow Up Work

Write *r-r-r-r*   *R-R-R-R*

r   R

rock

## Lesson VI

TEACHER: Let's add another letter to our collection tonight. It was taught to me this way: my teacher showed our class a picture like this. (Shows picture of cross cat f-f-f-ing at a dog.) She was about to tell us the sound the cat was making, but right away three or four boys in the class began saying "f-f-f-f" (sounds). She was pleased and told them they were exactly right. Then she wrote an "f" on the board. (Teacher writes "f") and said, "This letter always says just what the cross cat does." All of us found it easy to say it with her: "f-f-f-f." Now, class, if you will sound it with me, we can f-ind some f-words.

TEACHER AND CLASS: f-f-f-f (Sounds).

TEACHER: Good!

PUPIL (quickly): I know a word like that that we have had in our reading lessons—"f-ather."

TEACHER: Mr. Hawkins, I am really proud of that. It shows that you are watching out for all of the letters. Can any one think of other f-words?

FIRST PUPIL: "f-or" is one, isn't it?

SECOND PUPIL (simultaneously): "f-ind" and "f-ire" start that way.

TEACHER: Good! Class, let's say "f-ind" and "f-ire" together, holding on to the "f."

TEACHER AND CLASS TOGETHER: "f-ind," "f-ire."

PUPIL: I think this must be my letter because my last name is Farlow.

TEACHER: It certainly is, Mrs. F-arlow, and I'm so glad you claimed it. (Writes capital "F" on board.) Since it is your letter, won't you give us another f-word?

MRS. FARLOW: I was thinking of "f-uel."

TEACHER: Oh, thank you, Mrs. Farlow, for giving the very word that will help us make a good key sentence for "f": "F-ather will f-ind f-uel f-or the f-ire." Class, will you say that with me?

TEACHER AND CLASS: "F-ather will f-ind f-uel f-or the f-ire."

## Follow Up Work

Write *f-f-f-f*   *F-F-F-F*

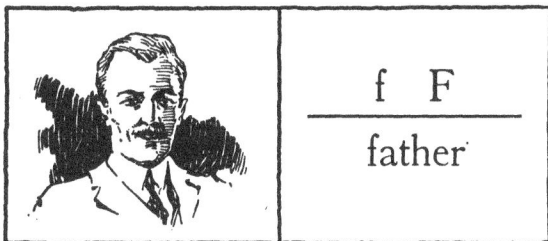

f   F
──────────
father

## Lesson VII

TEACHER: Class, what sounds have we been learning?

FIRST PUPIL: "l" (sounds).

SEVERAL PUPILS: "m" and "f" (sounds).

TEACHER: Will some one give me several l-words?

PUPIL: l-ike, l-ove, L-ena.

TEACHER: Good. Now, I'd like some m-words, please.

PUPIL: M-other, m-ade, m-e, m-y.

TEACHER: Good, again! Now, f-or our newest letter!

PUPIL: f-ather, f-ind, f-or.

TEACHER: In all of our collection of words, class, where have we f-ound the letters we are studying, at the beginning of the word, or at the end?

CLASS: They have been at the beginning of the words.

TEACHER: Good! Suppose now we find the same sounds at the end of some words. I'll give some first for you to guess. Which sound is at the end of "schoo-l"?

PUPILS: (No answer.)

TEACHER: Listen a minute, and I'll hold on to the last letter, while you decide whether I wind up the word with "l," "m," or "f." (Sounds these letters, then says "school-l-l.")

SEVERAL PUPILS: Why, it's "l," it doesn't end at all like "m" or "f."

TEACHER: Good! What about "pencil-l-l"?

SEVERAL PUPILS: That's "l" too.

TEACHER: Good! Now, you're getting the idea. With what sound does "from-m-m" end?

MARY: It ends with my letter, "m."

TEACHER: It does help to have a sound of our own, doesn't it? Before long, everybody in the class will have a sound that will be especially easy to remember, because it will belong to them. Now, tell me the sound at the end of "them-m-m."

PUPIL: That's the "m" sound again, isn't it?

TEACHER: Exactly! What about "him-m-m"?

SEVERAL PUPILS: Another "m"!

TEACHER: Yes, it is. Take "shall-l-l."

PUPIL: That goes back to "l."

TEACHER: Tell me about "will" and "well."

SEVERAL PUPILS: Both "l's."

TEACHER: Good. Now, just one more, "off-f-f."

PUPIL: That had to be "f" or "f" would have been left out, wouldn't it?

TEACHER: Mrs. F-arlow, do you remember the key sentence for your letter?

MRS. FARLOW: F-ather will f-ind f-uel f-or the f-ire.

TEACHER: Will all the women in the class whisper the key sentence?

WOMEN (whisper): F-ather will f-ind f-uel f-or the f-ire.

TEACHER: Will any of the men give us some new f-words?

ONE MAN: F-amily and f-unny.

SECOND MAN: f-ight.

THIRD MAN: f-ollow.

TEACHER: Good! Who will give a word that ends in "l"?

PUPIL: School.

PUPIL: Bell.

PUPIL: Will.

TEACHER: Very good! Now, please give us some words that end in "r" and some in "m."

PUPIL: Father, mother, brother, sister end with "r."

TEACHER: Nearly all of the family seem to end with "r," don't they? But even so, they may not be a growling family after all.

PUPIL: Them, from, and him end with "m."

TEACHER: You are all getting the sounds more quickly and giving them more clearly every night. Now, I am going to tell you the two stories about a new letter, just as they were told to me. One teacher told me that she saw a blacksmith put a hot horseshoe down in the water and it sounded just like this: s-s-s. Another teacher told our class that she was walking through the woods and was frightened when she saw a snake in her path and heard it make the sound, s-s-s. We thought both of these sounds were good for "s" (writes "s" on board), and I believe we didn't decide which was better. Will any one claim this letter before we go any further?

PUPIL: S-am and S-allie both ought to claim it, but they don't seem to be saying anything.

S-AM: You're right, but the funny thing is, it's yours, too, Mr. Smith, if I'm a good judge. (Laughter.) (Teacher writes capital "S" on board.)

MR. SMITH: I was a little too quick in looking out for the other fellow's business that time. But I'll claim the "s" all right and give you two "s" words besides the S-mith—s-ister and s-ee.

TEACHER: Good. Let's have about a half dozen "s" words.

PUPIL: S-ix and s-oon.

PUPIL: S-un and S-unday and s-chool.

TEACHER: Nearly every s-word you have given is either in a lesson we have had or in the new lessons ahead of us. And here they are in our type sentence: "S-ee my s-ix s-isters s-itting in the s-un." S-uppose we take "s-ister" for our type word. It has "s" at the beginning and also in the middle.

PUPIL: I have thought of two words that end with "s"—"this" and "yes."

TEACHER: Excellent! Will some one give us other words that end in "s"?

PUPILS: (No answer.)

TEACHER: I have thought of "likes," "takes," and "us." Now, will S-am and S-allie and Mr. S-mith repeat the type sentence for us?

SAM, SALLIE, AND MR. SMITH: "S-ee my s-ix s-isters s-itting in the s-un."

TEACHER: Good.   Now, will the class repeat it twice, the first time in a whisper, then aloud.

CLASS (Whispers): "S-ee my s-ix s-isters s-itting in the s-un."
(Aloud) "S-ee my s-ix s-isters s-itting in the s-un."

### Follow Up Work

Write s-s-s-s-s   S S S S S

s  S
sister

### Lesson VIII

Teacher's Note: In this and the following lessons, review sounds and letters that have been studied and teach the new ones indicated, following the general plan used in the first seven lessons, before teaching the phonograms.

New sounds and letters:
n—sound that a saw makes
p—motor boat sound

TEACHER: Class, have you ever thought why we are learning the sounds of the letters?  No one taught them to me until I was grown and was learning how to be a teacher.  But I had worked them out for myself, without knowing it.  I mean, if I heard the word "mother," I knew it began with "m."

PUPIL: Well, that's just what I didn't know.  The other day when you said "s-ister" real slowly and asked me what letter it began with, you surely did look surprised when I guessed "m." And that's when I began to see what it was all about.  If you know your beginning sounds, you can get a hold on your word to begin with and sort of work it out from that.

TEACHER: That's the idea, Mr. Cole, and after a while when you know all of the sounds you can puzzle out most of the words you find.

SECOND PUPIL: And the little I've learned so far is helping me out in another way.  I wish you could have heard my husband laughing at me yesterday.  He was sitting by the window reading, and I was just outside on the porch, writing.  Directly he came running out and said, "Lena, are you sick?"  And I said, "No, not at all. What made you think so?" "Because you were making such funny noises. I heard you go, m-m-m, f-f-f, r-r-r. If you're not sick, what's the matter?" And he certainly did laugh when I told him I was just blowing out some words that I wanted to spell. But it's my best help with the spelling just the same.

TEACHER: Mrs. Lawrence, I'm delighted that you have found that out already. And now that all of us know about fifty words, and some of our sounds, I believe we can learn something else that will help us puzzle out new words still more quickly and to spell them more easily. I am thinking of word families. We are used to thinking of people in families, aren't we? Suppose I write on the board the names of all of the members of Mr. White's family. (Writes)

> Tom White
> Mary White
> Bob White
> Ann White

If I cover up the first names, you see only the family name—"White"—all the way down the list, don't you? And it is the same way with word families. Suppose we take the "at" family because there is an "at" word in our lesson to-day. (Writes)

> at
> m at
> r at
> f at
> s at
> p at
> N at

If I cover up the first names of this family, what do you see all the way down?

PUPILS: at.

TEACHER: Will you say it as many times as you see it?

PUPIL: at, at, at, at, at, at, at.

TEACHER: Good! Now, for the first names. I have written letters that we can sound. So let's see what is the first member of this word family. I'll say it slowly and you can guess it—"m-at."

PUPIL: Mat, isn't it?

TEACHER: That's exactly what it is. Now listen to the next: "R-at."

SEVERAL PUPILS: Rat!

TEACHER: Good! Then what is "f-at"?

SEVERAL PUPILS: "Fat," and the others are "sat," "pat," and "Nat."

TEACHER: That is even better than I expected. And we have used all of the letters that we have studied except "l." If I say "lat," will that make a word?

SEVERAL PUPILS: No.

ONE PUPIL: Yes, ma'am, it will make my name, won't it? Lat Davis is my name.

TEACHER: Good enough, Mr. Davis. I have never known any one named Lat before and I am glad to have you finish up the family group for us. (Writes Lat.) I wonder if you can read the names of all of your "at" family group for us?

MR. DAVIS: at, mat, rat, fat, sat, pat, and I don't believe I know the next one before Lat.

TEACHER: That is another man's name, Nat, and that is why it is written with a capital. Suppose, class, we read the "at" family group again.

TEACHER AND PUPILS: at, mat, rat, fat, sat, pat, Nat, Lat.

TEACHER: Good! Now, whenever you see a word that has "at" in it, you will know that much of the word right away. Let's turn to the reading lesson and see which member of the "at" family is there.

SEVERAL PUPILS: It is "at" itself.

TEACHER: Good! Suppose we write, "Lat and Nat are fat" for our type sentence. Tomorrow, please be able to call the roll of the "at" family. And Mr. Davis, we shall expect you to give the first roll call.

### Follow Up Work

Write list of "at" family.

Copy: "Nat and Lat are fat."

## Lesson IX

k—choking sound

w—the wind sound

qu—kw

TEACHER: Mr. L-at Davis, we've been looking forward to your calling the roll of the "at" family. Are you ready to begin now?

MR. DAVIS: I've had nearly everybody in the settlement listen to me while I called them over at different times, so I think I ought to be ready:

at

m-at

r-at

f-at

s-at

p-at

N-at

L-at

TEACHER: Perfect, Mr. Davis. Will some one else say as many as possible of this "at" family?

PUPIL: N-at, r-at, f-at, N-at, L-at.

SECOND PUPIL: He left out "at" itself, and yesterday I thought of two others, "c-at" and "h-at."

TEACHER: Good work! I didn't put "c-at" and "h-at" in the list because we hadn't studied those sounds, but they certainly are members of the "at" family and I'm delighted that you thought of them. Now, class, let's give the names of all of the "ats" we know.

TEACHER AND CLASS: at, m-at, r-at, f-at, s-at, p-at, N-at and L-at, c-at, h-at.

TEACHER: Good! Now, let's try another family group. Writes:

> moth-er
> fath-er
> sist-er
> broth-er
> lett-er

You know all of these words, so please read them for me.

CLASS: Mother, father, sister, brother, letter.

TEACHER: Who will tell me the family name of this group?

CLASS: (No answer.)

TEACHER: Suppose I cover up all of the first names (covers them). What do you see all the way down the list? Please say it as many times as you see it.

CLASS: Er, er, er, er, er.

TEACHER: Good! Now what is the name of this family?

CLASS: The "er" family.

TEACHER: Now, you have it! Suppose we look in our reading lesson for tonight and see how many members of the "er" family are there.

FIRST PUPIL: I see moth-er and fath-er.

SECOND PUPIL: And in the very next sentence, I see sist-er and broth-er.

THIRD PUPIL: I see something but I don't know whether it is exactly in that family or not. In the first sentence, I see a word that has "er" in the middle of it. Can we bring that into the family group?

TEACHER: Good for you, Mrs. Ownbey! I didn't expect any one to find that one until we had studied many more groups. What is the word?

MRS. OWNBEY: Ev-er-y.

TEACHER: Yes, and it is certainly in the "er" family, isn't it, class? Now, will you call the roll?

CLASS: Moth-er, fath-er, sist-er, broth-er, lett-er, and ev-er-y.

TEACHER: Good! Now, we've studied two families, let's see if we really know them when they are not all together. (Writes a column containing words from each group.)

mat
mother
father
rat
sister
brother
fat

Now, who will come and check all of the "at" words?

PUPIL: I see three "at" words there. (Checks them.)

TEACHER: Good! Then what words are left?

PUPIL: There are four "er" words.

TEACHER: Good! For the type sentence, let's write: "Mother and father see sister and brother." In our next reading lesson there is an "at" word and there are five "er" words. I shall certainly be interested in seeing who can show them to me on Thursday evening.

### Follow Up Work

Write three "er" words.

Copy: "Mother and father see sister and brother."

## Lesson X

c—choking sound
k—choking sound
c (s)—another hissing sound
x—ks

PUPIL: I found "at" twice and the five "er" words in tonight's lesson.

TEACHER: Good! I told one of my friends to-day that I did hope everybody would remember to look up those family words. when we come to them. When we know the parts of a new word, we don't have to swallow it whole but can take one bite at a time.

SEVERAL PUPILS: Moth-er, fath-er, sist-er, broth-er, and ev-er-y.

TEACHER: That is excellent. Can any one repeat the type sentence for the "at" family?

PUPIL: If I can just take one look in the book to see how it starts, I can say it without any trouble.

TEACHER: All right, Mr. Buckner, take one quick look.

MR. BUCKNER: (Looks in book) Of course! "Lat and Nat are fat."

TEACHER: Good. Monday night, I'm going to ask you to give us the "at" sentence *without* looking in the book at all. Now, who remembers the "er" sentence?

PUPILS: (No answer.)

TEACHER: What are some of the "er" words?

SEVERAL PUPILS: Mother, father, sister, brother.

PUPIL: Oh, yes, the sentence is: "Mother and father see sister and brother."

TEACHER: Good! Now, class, let's give first the "at" sentence, then the "er" sentence.

TEACHER AND CLASS: "Lat and Nat are fat."
"Mother and father see sister and brother."

TEACHER: Tonight we want to become acquainted with another word family. It is a large family with a short name, "ay." I shall write it eight times. (Writes)

| ay | ay |
|----|----|
| ay | ay |
| ay | ay |
| ay | ay |

Now, let's try the sounds which we know with this family name and see how many words we can find that belong there. What is "l-ay"?

CLASS: Lay.

TEACHER: And m-ay?

CLASS: May.

TEACHER: All right, as I sound the word and you blend it, I shall write it down. (Writes)

| l ay | p ay |
|------|------|
| m ay | s ay |
| r ay | n ay |
| f ay | w ay |

Let's say all eight of them, holding on to the first sound and then saying the family name.

TEACHER AND CLASS:

| l ay | p ay |
|------|------|
| m ay | s ay |
| r ay | n ay |
| f ay | w ay |

TEACHER: Now, let's blend them and say them just as we do in talking.

TEACHER AND CLASS:

| lay | pay |
|-----|-----|
| may | say |
| ray | nay |
| fay | way |

PUPIL: I can understand all of them except "fay." Is that a regular word?

TEACHER: Good for you, Mr. Ingle. That shows you are really thinking about these words. Yes, "fay" is a regular word, but it is one that we don't use very often. We have all heard of fairies, haven't we? "Fay" is just another way of saying "fairy." There is another one of the "ay" words that I'd like for us to think about—ray. Sometimes we speak of a ray of light, don't we? That's one kind of ray. Then, did you ever know any one named Ray?

PUPIL: My boy's name is Ray.

TEACHER: That is interesting because I want to use Ray as some one's name in our type sentence. What do you think of this: "Ray may pay our way."

PUPIL: I think that will be easy to remember because we like to think some one may pay our way.

TEACHER: Good. I hope everybody will remember. And I shall want to hear at our next lesson the "at" sentence, the "er" sentence and the "ay" sentence.

## Lesson XI

Teacher's Note: In all of the following lessons, whenever time permits, give short spirited review of consonant sounds, previously learned.

t—the watch sound
d—the dove sound

Teacher's Note: Give this sound accurately. Do not say "duh" nor "der." Try it at the end of many words as well as at the beginning.

TEACHER: How many can give the "at," "er," and "ay" sentences, all three? (A number of hands raised.) Good for you! Everybody take part and give them in concert.

PUPILS: Lat and Nat are fat.
Mother and father see sister and brother.
Ray may pay our way.

TEACHER: Perfect, and nearly everybody took part. Mrs. Frady (pupil who did not join in second sentence), will you give us the "er" sentence?

MRS. FRADY: I can give it now, but I had to wait for them to start me off: Mother and father see sister and brother.

TEACHER: Good work! Now, I'm wondering if we should know that a new word is an "er" word even before we know what the word is. Turn to the reading lesson for tonight. (Class opens books.) In the second sentence, there is an "er" word and it is not an easy word either. Does any one see it?

MANY PUPILS: It is the last word in the line.

TEACHER: Good! Now, the first sentence is, "My wife and I have a son." The second one is, "My wife and I have a—"

PUPILS: Daughter.

TEACHER: Good! Then what is the new "er" word?

CLASS: It's "daughter".

TEACHER: Good! Now, let's do a little more pioneering. Look at the third sentence in Lesson XII. Does any one see an "er" word there?

PUPIL: Yes, it's the last one again and a long one.

TEACHER: Exactly. We don't know what it is, but we know it ends in "er." Let's do a little guessing. I'll read the first two sentences and all but the last word in the third. (Reads)

> My husband reads to me.
> I like for him to read to me.
> He likes to read the ——.

PUPIL: Paper.

TEACHER: That's part of it. Let's find "paper" in the word. We know "er" don't we? What letter is just before "er" and how does it sound?

CLASS: It is "p" and sounds "p" (sound it).

TEACHER: Then what is "p-er"?

CLASS: It's "per."

TEACHER: Good. I'll sound the two letters that come just before "per." (Sounds) "p," "a" (long).

SEVERAL PUPILS: That sounds "pa" (long) and that gives us our "pa-per."

TEACHER: That is good. Now what kind of a paper do you think the man likes to read?

PUPIL: He likes to read a newspaper.

TEACHER: Just exactly—"newspaper." Now when you come to that long word in tomorrow's lesson, you will already know that it is ————

CLASS: Newspaper.

### Follow Up Work

Write two "at" words, two "er" words, and two "ay" words.

## Lesson XII

h—the tired letter
s and z—the buzzing letters

TEACHER: Sometimes it seems that there are so many, many things that must be learned before we can read well, doesn't it? But isn't it a comfort to remember that there are only twenty-six letters that have to be learned? When we know those twenty-six, we know every single letter in our language. And sixteen of them always have the same sound. Whenever we see b, d, f, h, j, k, l, m, n, p, q, r, t, v, x and z, we know that they are going to sound exactly the same way. And three of the other letters have only two sounds.  You know two of these letters that have only two sounds.  Do you remember which two they are?

PUPIL: We've just been studying one of them tonight, "s." Sometimes it hisses and sometimes it buzzes.

TEACHER: Good for you, Mr. Hollingsworth!  Can't some one think of the other one?

PUPILS: (No answer.)

TEACHER: Don't you remember we studied it in our last lesson. And I've thought of something else that may help us remember it. Mr. Hollingsworth has just said that sometimes "s" hisses and sometimes it buzzes.  Well, this other letter sometimes hisses and sometimes chokes.

SEVERAL PUPILS: Of course we know now.  It is "c."

TEACHER: Exactly.  And the other letter that has only two sounds is "g."  Both of its sounds are hard to make, but we are going to learn one of them in our next lesson.  Now, let's try a little arithmetic.  How many letters are there in our language?

CLASS: There are only twenty-six.

TEACHER: How many have only one sound?

CLASS: (No answer.)

TEACHER: I'll put that number on the board and the letters too.  That will help us remember them, won't it?  (Makes the number 16 and writes the sixteen consonants.)  When we have learned them, we have learned them once for all.  Now, class, how many of the letters have only one sound?

CLASS: Sixteen of them have only one sound.

PUPIL: It surely is a comfort to know that.  It's the best encouragement I've had, because we already know a good many of them.

TEACHER: You are right, Mr. Harris.  It *is* encouraging to know that in only a dozen lessons, we have learned so large a part of all the sounds that we shall ever have to know.  Now, let's get back to our number questions again.  How many letters have only two sounds?

PUPIL: "c," "s" and "g" have only two sounds.

TEACHER: Exactly right.  The 16 letters that have only one sound and the 3 letters that have only two sounds are called consonants.  If there are 19 consonants, how many letters are left that we haven't talked about yet?

PUPIL: 16 and 3 make 19, and 19 from 26 leaves 7.

TEACHER: Good for you, Mr. Martin.  Now, we are ready to talk about those 7.  They are called vowels.  I wonder who can name them?

PUPIL: I can think of "a," "i" and "o."

TEACHER: That is a good beginning.  We usually name the vowels this way: a, e, i, o, u and sometimes w and y.  We say "sometimes w and y" because sometimes these two letters are consonants and sometimes they are vowels. We shall study them later on. Tonight we want to talk about a, e, i, o and u. (Writes them on board.) Each of them has a number of sounds but we are going to drill on just two of these—the long sound and the short sound. And tonight we are going to try out only the long sounds. We are taking the long sounds first because they are so easy to learn. The long sounds are just exactly like the names of the letters. I mean that when "a" is long, it sounds "a" as in "ate," "name," "baby." Can any one think of another word that has an "a" in it that sounds just like the name of the letter—"a"?

CLASS: (No answer.)

TEACHER: I have thought of one—"take." Can't you think of one that rhymes with "take"?

FIRST PUPIL: Make.

SECOND PUPIL: Bake and rake.

THIRD PUPIL: Sake and fake and lake.

TEACHER: Excellent. Now, long "e" sounds just like its name, too. Here are some words with long "e" in them: "eat," "me," "be." Can you give me one or two words that rhyme with "me" and "be"?

PUPIL: "she" and "the" rhyme with "me" and "be."

TEACHER: Good. Next let's think of some words with long "i." I think of "ice," "mice," "like" and "fight." Give me some words that rhyme with "fight."

FIRST PUPIL: "Tight" and "light."

SECOND PUPIL: "Might" and "night" and "right."

TEACHER: You are getting quickly the idea of these long vowel sounds. Now, for the long "o." I have thought of "old" and "fold," and "told."

PUPIL: I have thought of "bold" and "cold" and "hold."

TEACHER: Our last sound for tonight is "u." I am thinking of "use" and "union" and "sure." What are your words for long "u"?

FIRST PUPIL: "Pure" and "cure."

SECOND PUPIL: "Music" and "fuel."

TEACHER: Excellent. This has been a splendid lesson, class. What do we call these five letters that have so many different sounds?

CLASS: (No answer.)

TEACHER: I will write it on the board. (Writes "Vowels.") We call them vowels and we call the other letters consonants (Writes "Consonants." Let's say the two words together.

TEACHER AND CLASS: "Vowels" and "Consonants."

TEACHER: For our type sentence, let's try this: "Amy eats ice and oatmeal and uses uniforms." We may remember it because it is not a very serious sentence. (Class repeats.)

### Follow Up Work

Copy 19 consonants. Copy 5 vowels. Copy 2 letters that are sometimes vowels and sometimes consonants.

## Lesson XIII

v—trolley car sound
g—gargling sound

TEACHER: What three word families have we studied?

PUPIL: We have studied the "at," "er" and "ay" families.

TEACHER: What consonants have we studied?

FIRST PUPIL: I can think of l, m, r, f, two s's and z. (Teacher writes each letter as sound is given.)

SECOND PUPIL: I remember p, n, w, two c's and k. (Teacher writes.)

THIRD PUPIL: Just lately we have had t, d and h. (Teacher writes.)

FOURTH PUPIL: And tonight we drilled on v and g. (Teacher writes.)

TEACHER: Excellent! Now, I am going to put on the board the name of another family. (Writes "ake.") It is the "ake" family. I shall write it nine times. See if you can think of nine members of the "ake" family. Look at the list of letters that we have learned how to sound, and try them with "ake" to see if they will make words.

SEVERAL PUPILS: lake, make, rake, fake.

PUPIL: sake and wake.

PUPIL: take and cake.

TEACHER: And quake! Now, we have nine members of the "ake" family and you found all of them but one. I believe you can make the type sentence, too. Who will try?

PUPILS: (No answer.)

TEACHER: Suppose we begin, "Take the rake."

PUPIL: "Take the rake down to the lake."

TEACHER: Very good indeed. Suppose we repeat that "ake" sentence together.

TEACHER AND CLASS: "Take the rake down to the lake."

TEACHER: Does any one remember what we call the letters that are not consonants and that have several different sounds?

CLASS: (No answer.)

TEACHER: We call them vowels. (Writes "vowels" on the board.) We are going to speak so often of vowels and consonants that we want to be sure which are which. Can any one name the five long vowel sounds?

PUPILS: (No answer.)

TEACHER: "Amy eats—"
SEVERAL PUPILS: "Amy eats ice and oatmeal and uses uniforms."
TEACHER: Then what are the long vowel sounds?
SEVERAL PUPILS: a, e, i, o, u.

### Follow Up Work

Copy the five vowels. Copy the type sentence for the five long vowel sounds.

## Lesson XIV

y—mouse-in-trap sound (consonant)
y—like i (vowel)
w—like u (vowel)
b—baby sound

TEACHER: Who can give the type sentence for the long vowels?
PUPIL: "Amy eats ice and oatmeal and uses uniforms."
TEACHER: Good. Who will give the word in that sentence that has long "a" in it?
PUPIL: Amy.
TEACHER: Can any one think of some other word that begins with long "a"?
PUPIL: Ape.
TEACHER: Good! Which word in the type sentence begins with long "o"?
PUPIL: Oatmeal begins with long "o."
TEACHER: That is right. Will some one give us another word that begins with long "o"?
PUPIL: Old begins with long "o" and cold and bold and sold have a long "o" in the middle.
TEACHER: Excellent! I wasn't sure whether we could recognize them yet unless they were at the beginning.
TEACHER: Suppose we look in our reading lesson for a word with long "o." (Books opened to Lesson XIV.) Look in the very first sentence. The first "o" we come to is in "our." Is that long?
CLASS: No, that's not long.
TEACHER: The next "o" is in "to." What about that? Say it over to yourself. Then say "o" (long sound) and see what you think about it.
SEVERAL PUPILS: No, that "o" is not long.
TEACHER: Good! The next "o" is in "go."
CLASS: That's a long one!
TEACHER: It certainly is. Now, we have another "to" and then "school"—sch-oo-l. Are those two o's like one long one?

CLASS: No, they are different.

TEACHER: Good. Now, let's do some pioneering. Turn to Lesson XVIII and look at the second sentence. Look at next to the last word. The "o" in that word is long and the "e" makes no sound at all. It is silent. Now, let's sound the letters as we come to them and see what that word is.

TEACHER AND CLASS: N-o-t-e. (Sound first three letters.)

PUPIL: It is "note," isn't it?

TEACHER: It surely is note. Now, we shall be just that much ahead when we come to the eighteenth lesson. We shall know "note." Suppose we just read the sentence as you know all of the other words but one. The third word is "word." Who will read the sentence.

SEVERAL PUPILS: "Write the word in your notebook."

TEACHER: Excellent. In the first sentence in Lesson XIX, I see a good word for us to puzzle out. It is the fourth word and the "o" is long. Do you recognize any other part of it?

SEVERAL PUPILS: It belongs to the "er" family!

TEACHER: It surely does. Now, let's try out the other sounds, as we know all of them.

TEACHER AND CLASS: P-o-s-t-er.

SEVERAL PUPILS: It is poster!

TEACHER: Exactly! Very soon now, we can look at every new word in our reading lessons and find that we know some, if not all, of the parts of it, can't we?

### Follow Up Work

Write one word for each of the long vowels.

## Lesson XV

j—dzh
g—dzh

TEACHER: We've been working with the long vowels and tonight I thought we might look at both the long and short ones. I shall write some words on the board in pairs. You may not know what the words are, but please be ready to tell me in what they are alike and in what they are different from each other. (Writes)

| at | ate | not | note |
| can | cane | rob | robe |
| hid | hide | us | use |
| bit | bite | cut | cute |

PUPIL: The pairs are exactly alike except that one of them has an "e" on the end.

TEACHER: That is just what I hoped you would notice. Now, as I read them, please see if you can tell in which one of the words of the pairs the middle vowel has the long sound. Is it the one that has the "e" on the end or the one that hasn't? (Reads all eight of the word pairs stopping after each pair to find out which is long.)

SEVERAL PUPILS: The long sounds are in the words that have "e" on the end.

TEACHER: Exactly. Now, I believe if I give the first word— the one that has the short sound—you can give the second word of each pair, even though these are practically all new words to you. Let's try them.

TEACHER: at.

CLASS: ate.

TEACHER: can.

CLASS: cane.

(and so on through the list)

PUPIL: Those pairs have all five of the vowels in the middle of them, except "e," haven't they?

TEACHER: Good for you, Mr. Ledford! Not one pupil in a thousand would have noticed that. I left it out because the words that I thought of for "e" happened not to be quite as easy as those for the other vowels. But I am delighted that you missed the "e" and called for it. We must write two pairs for it just as for the others. (Writes)

|      |      |
|------|------|
| met  | mete |
| pet  | Pete | (Reads them)

"Mete" is a word that we don't use very often. But perhaps you have heard the expression, "to mete out justice." It means to measure. In the second pair, why did I begin "Pete" with a capital?

PUPIL: It begins with a capital because it is somebody's name.

TEACHER: Good! Now suppose we put the "e" pairs in their natural place just after the "a" pairs, and then read all of them. (Writes pairs in place.)

TEACHER AND CLASS:

| at  | ate  | hid | hide | us  | use  |
|-----|------|-----|------|-----|------|
| can | cane | bit | bite | cut | cute |
| met | mete | not | note |     |      |
| pet | Pete | rob | robe |     |      |

TEACHER: Very good! Now, in the few minutes left, let's see if we can find some of the members of a new family—not an easy family name either. (Writes "ight.") I shall write it seven times. (Writes.) Will you repeat it as many times as you see it?

CLASS: ight, ight, ight, ight, ight, ight, ight.

TEACHER: How many letters are there in "ight"?

CLASS: There are four letters in it.

TEACHER: Listen while I pronounce it slowly and see if you can tell me how many sounds there are in it. (Pronounces, "i g h t.")

SEVERAL PUPILS: There are two sounds.

TEACHER: Can any one tell me what are the two sounds in "ight"?

PUPIL: The two sounds that I hear are "i" and "t." (Sounds both.)

TEACHER: Very good. Now, as fast as you will tell me the consonant sounds that we have learned, I will write them on the board. You make the sound and I'll write the letter. Then we can look at them and see which ones will help us with the "ight" family.

PUPIL: We've had just about all of them now, haven't we? So we can just come down the a, b, c's, leaving out the vowels.

TEACHER: That is excellent, Mrs. Watkins. So class, please begin with "b" and tell me all of the consonants. (Class gives sounds and teacher writes the letters.)

| b | g | l | q | v | z |
|---|---|---|---|---|---|
| c | h | m | r | w |   |
| d | j | n | s | x |   |
| f | k | p | t | y |   |

PUPIL: "Fight" is the first one I see.

TEACHER: Very good indeed.

FIRST PUPIL: Then I see "light," "might" and "night."

SECOND PUPIL: And I see "right," "sight" and "tight."

TEACHER: There, class, we have our seven "ight" words. And when we learn some of the blends, we can add still more to this family. We can have words like "bright," "blight" and "fright." But we have surely covered enough ground for to*night* and we must stop here.

### Follow Up Work

Copy the word-pairs with the long and the short vowels in them.

## Lesson XVI

Teacher's Note: Give short spirited drill on sounds of b, c, d, f, g, h, j, k, l, m, n, p, q, r, s, t, v, w, x, y, z.

TEACHER: Does any one remember our type sentence for the long vowels? It begins with "Amy."

SEVERAL PUPILS: "Amy eats ice and oatmeal and uses uniforms."

PUPIL: My daughter heard me saying that sentence last night and she said she believed Amy must have been a trained nurse. (Laughter.)

TEACHER: I feel sure that she was and now she is helping train us, isn't she? Let's see if she has really helped us remember what the long vowel sounds are. All who can, give them.

CLASS: a, e, i, o, u.

TEACHER: Perfect! I believe we know them now and I'm glad because tonight we want to learn the short sounds of the vowels. Let's see what we remember about the word pairs that had some long and some short vowel sounds.

FIRST PUPIL: I remember that the pairs were just alike except that one of them had an "e" at the end.

SECOND PUPIL: I remember that the one that had the "e" at the end had a long vowel sound in the middle.

TEACHER: Class, that is excellent and much more than I expected you to remember from that one lesson. I will write the pairs on the board again. (Writes.)

| | | | | | |
|---|---|---|---|---|---|
| at | ate | hid | hide | us | use |
| can | cane | bit | bite | cut | cute |
| met | mete | not | note | | |
| pet | Pete | rob | robe | | |

Now, that we know the long sounds of the vowels, let's see if we can puzzle out the short sounds. Beginning with "a," listen while I sound "a-t." What was the first sound I made?

CLASS: "a" (Give short sound.)

TEACHER: Good. In the next word there are three sounds. See if you can hear the short "a." (Sounds c-a-n.)

PUPIL: Yes, "a" is the second sound.

TEACHER: Good. Now, let's see if we can think of some other words that begin with "a" (short sound).

PUPIL: Don't "am" and "add" begin with short "a"?

TEACHER: They surely do. Can any one think of other "a" words?

PUPIL: I have thought of "an," "and," and "animal."

TEACHER: Very good indeed. I will write your "a" words here in a column. (Writes.)

am
add
an
and
animal

Now, let's find out how "e" sounds when it is short. Our two "e" words in the list are "met" and "pet." Listen closely while

I sound them: (sounds "m-e-t," "p-e-t"). Can you tell me how the "e" sounds in these words?

PUPIL: It sounds "e" (gives short sound).

TEACHER: Excellent. Now, let's think of some words that begin with the "e" sound, if we can. Somehow, I always think of "egg," so I'll write that first (writes). Can any one give me some other "e" words?

CLASS: (No answer.)

TEACHER: I am thinking of a very large animal with a trunk and two tusks.

CLASS: Elephant.

TEACHER: I am thinking of a box that is not full but is—?

SEVERAL PUPILS: Empty.

TEACHER: I am thinking not of the beginning of my journey but of the—?

CLASS: End!

TEACHER: Good. I will write these "e" words. (Writes "elephant," "empty" and "end" under "egg.") Now, let's say them together, holding on to the "e" sound, and then give the "e" sound four times.

TEACHER AND CLASS: e-gg, e-lephant, e-mpty, e-nd, e, e, e, e.

TEACHER: That brings us to short "i," doesn't it? And our words are "h-i-d" and "b-i-t."

PUPIL: Then short "i" sounds "i," and I've thought of "i-t."

TEACHER: Excellent. We are beginning on the i's splendidly. Who will give us other words that begin with "i"? (Sounds.)

FIRST PUPIL: I have thought of "if," "is" and "ill."

SECOND PUPIL: And I have thought of "in" and "inch."

TEACHER: Very good indeed. Now, I'll write the "i" words. (Writes "it," "is," "if," "ill," "in" and "inch.") And that brings us to the next to the last of the vowels that we are studying— short "o." When I sound the words from the list, I believe you will know what the sound of short "o" is. (Sounds "n-o-t" and "r-o-b.")

PUPIL: It sounds "o" (gives short sound).

TEACHER: I have thought of "offer" and "office."

PUPIL: And I have thought of "odd" and "olive."

TEACHER: I will write the "o" words that we have thought of all in a row: "offer," "office," "odd" and "olive." Suppose we ask the women to repeat these words with me.

TEACHER AND WOMEN: "offer," "office," "odd" and "olive."

TEACHER: Now, we have only the "u" sound to work on. From our list we get "u-s" and "c-u-t." Will the men make the short sound of "u"?

MEN: "u" (give short sound).

FIRST PUPIL: One word that begins with "u" is "up."

Second Pupil: And "under" is one that begins with "u".

Third Pupil: And I have thought of "ugly" and "umpire."

Teacher: I am delighted with the work you have done tonight. (Writes "up," "under," "ugly," "umpire.") I have never had a class before that managed to get these short sounds as quickly as you have. Now, let's work out a type sentence for these short sounds. What do you think of this: "An elephant is odd and ugly"?

## Lesson XVII

Teacher: Class, will you give me the type sentence for the long vowel sounds?

Class: "Amy eats ice and oatmeal and uses uniforms."

Teacher: Good! Will you give the long vowel sounds?

Class: a, e, i, o, u (long sounds).

Teacher: Will you give the type sentence for the short vowel sounds?

Several Pupils: "An elephant is odd and ugly."

Teacher: Very good. Will you give the short vowel sounds?

Class: a, e, i, o, u (short sounds).

Slow Pupil: How do these sentences help you remember the sounds? They seem to help everybody else but I can't see the connection.

Teacher: I am so glad you asked that question, Mrs. Brown. I don't believe we have ever once said just how those sentences are meant to help us. Will someone explain how they do help?

Pupil: Why, the first letter of each word gives you the sound you want to remember. In the sentence for the long vowels, "Amy" begins with "a"; "eats" begins with "e"; "ice" begins with "i." Then we just have to throw in the "and" to join them together. "Oatmeal" begins with "o." Then we need another "and" for joining purposes. And "uses" and "uniforms" both begin with "u." Those "ands" might mix you up a little, but, you see, you already know the sounds and you just want something to bring them back to mind. So when you say, "Amy eats ice and oatmeal and uses uniforms," you get your a, e, i, o, u in mind.

Teacher: Very good indeed, Mrs. Bates. Now can any one explain the sentence for the short vowel sounds?

Pupil: The sentence is, "An elephant is odd and ugly." The first sound of each word is one of the short vowel sounds. We pass over the "and" because we know it just joins the others together. "An" begins with "a"; "elephant" begins with "e"; "is" begins with "i"; "odd" begins with "o"; and "ugly" begins with "u." So when we say, "An elephant is odd and ugly," it is easy to remember a, e, i, o, u (short sounds).

MRS. BROWN: It seems funny that I didn't think of that for myself. But I didn't and I won't forget it.

TEACHER: Mrs. Brown, I expect there are others who didn't just understand about the sentences, and I am very glad indeed that you gave us this opportunity to explain them. Now, won't you choose one of the short sounds and ask some one to give you a word that has that sound in it? It won't matter in what part of the word the short sound is. It may, or may not, be at the beginning of the word.

MRS. BROWN: Will some one give a word that has the "a" (short) sound in it?

FIRST PUPIL: "Am" begins with "a" (short sound).

SECOND PUPIL: "Back" and "tack" have the "a" sound in them.

TEACHERS Good. Now, I am going to ask the President of the Class, the Secretary, the Treasurer, and the Chairman of the Recreation Committee, each to choose a short vowel sound and ask for a word that contains it.

PRESIDENT: Who will give me a word that has "u" (short sound) in it?

PUPIL: "umpire" begins with "u" (short sound).

SECRETARY: I'd like a word for the "o" sound (short), please.

PUPIL: "Box" has the "o" sound in it.

TREASURER: The short sound I choose is "e." Who will give me a word?

PUPIL: "Nest" and "pest" have the "e" sound in them.

CHAIRMAN: The short sound that is left for me is "i." Please give me two or three words with that sound in them.

PUPIL: "In," "is," and "it" have "i" (short) in them.

TEACHER: That was splendid work, class. Now, suppose we investigate a few of the words in tonight's reading lesson to see whether we can find any long and short vowels in them. (Books are opened to Lesson XVII.) I will sound the words and you decide whether the vowels in them are long or short. Some of them won't be either long or short, because as you remember, the vowels have several sounds. But we won't stop now to drill on any of the sounds except the long and the short. Of course, if you happen to remember any of the others that we find, so much the better. Let's try the words in the first sentence. As I sound each word, you call out, "Long," "short," or "neither." "W-e" (sounds).

CLASS: Long.

TEACHER: "Sh-a-ll."

SEVERAL PUPILS: Short.

TEACHER: "H-a-v-e."

CLASS: Short.

TEACHER: "a."

CLASS: Long.

TEACHER: Which are easier to be sure of, class, the long or the short sounds?

PUPIL: The long sounds are easier to be sure of, because the long sounds are just like the names of the letters.

TEACHER: Good! The next word is "n-ight."

CLASS: Long.

TEACHER: "Sch-oo-l."

ONE PUPIL: Neither.

TEACHER: Good. Two o's together have a different sound. The last word is "p-ar-ty."

SEVERAL PUPILS: Neither.

TEACHER: Very good, indeed. Now, let's wind up this excellent lesson by repeating first the long sounds of the vowels and then the short sounds.

CLASS: a, e, i, o, u (long sounds).

a, e, i, o, u (short sounds).

### Follow Up Work

Find a word in your reader that has a long "a" in it. Copy this word in your notebook.

Find a word in your reader that has a short "a" in it. Copy this word in your notebook.

## Lesson XVIII

Teacher's note: Give short, spirited drill on "b," "d," "g," "j," and "y."

TEACHER: Suppose you were trying to hear what a friend was saying and the children made so much noise that you couldn't understand what your friend was saying. What would you say to the children?

SEVERAL PUPILS: "Sh! sh!"

TEACHER: Good. I'll write "sh" on the board (writes). Some of the letters work together in making sounds. They blend together just as "s" and "h" do here and make one blended sound, "sh." This blend may be at the beginning of a word, as in "shall." It may be at the end of a word, as in "hush." Or it may be found in the middle of a word as in "brushing." But always it sounds the same way. How does it sound, class?

CLASS: "Sh! Sh!"

TEACHER: Exactly. Now, let's make a collection of "sh" words. As fast as you give them to me, I will write them on the board.

FIRST PUPIL: "She" and "shall."

SECOND PUPIL: "Should" and "show."

THIRD PUPIL: "Shout" and "short."

FOURTH PUPIL: "Shepherd."

TEACHER: Excellent. Now, Mrs. Brown, suppose we make a type sentence for "sh." In this sentence, we shall have as many of the words as possible begin with "sh." Suppose we use some of the words given by the class. How will this do: "Shall she shout to the short shepherd?" Don't you think there are enough "sh's" there to fix it in our minds? Will you repeat it?

MRS. BROWN: "Shall she shout to the short shepherd?"

TEACHER: Good! Now, let's work on another blend. Suppose when we get outside tonight, a strong icy wind blows hard against us. What shall we probably say as we button up our coats more tightly?

CLASS: (No answer.)

TEACHER: Why, I can almost hear you now, saying, "br, br, br" as that cold wind strikes you. (Laughter.) That sound is made by "b" and "r" working together. Will you make the sound as I write the blend? (Writes "br.")

CLASS: "Br! Br!" (Sounds.)

TEACHER: Good. Now, for some "br" words. I'll begin with "brave." (Writes.)

FIRST PUPIL: "Brother."

SECOND PUPIL: "Bread" and "bran."

THIRD PUPIL: "Break."

FOURTH PUPIL: "Broad."

TEACHER: Excellent. And our "br" sentence can be: "Brave brothers break bread together." Let's all repeat it.

TEACHER AND CLASS: Now, suppose we leave the blends for the present and work up a large family word group. It is the "ing" family. Suppose I write it a dozen times and see if we can't find at least that many "ing" words. (Writes.)

| | | | |
|---|---|---|---|
| ing | ing | ing | ing |
| ing | ing | ing | ing |
| ing | ing | ing | ing |
| ing | ing | ing | ing |

FIRST PUPIL: "Ring" and "sing" are "ing" words, aren't they? (Teacher writes.)

TEACHER: They surely are.

SECOND PUPIL: "Thing" and "spring" and "string." (Teacher writes.)

THIRD PUPIL: "Bring" and "wing" and "king."

TEACHER: Excellent. Now, for our other four words. Suppose we add another "ing" to some of the words you've just given; as, "ringing," "singing," "bringing," and "springing." There are many, many words that end in "ing." So when you see it, what will you know that part of the word is?

CLASS: "Ing."

TEACHER: Suppose we take for our type sentence for "ing": "The king will bring a ring." Will you repeat that?
CLASS: "The king will bring a ring."

### Follow Up Work

Write "ing" in your notebook. Under it, copy the sentence: "The king will bring a ring."

## Lesson XIX

TEACHER: What do I mean when I speak of a blend, class?
CLASS: (No answer.)
TEACHER: Can you think of the blend that quiets the children?
SEVERAL PUPILS: "Sh."
TEACHER: Good. And what is the blend that a cold, icy wind makes us say?
SEVERAL PUPILS: "Br! Br!"
TEACHER: Exactly. "Sh" and "br" are the two blends we have studied. When two or more letters work together, as these do, to make a blended sound, we call it a blend, don't we? There are many blends which we shall learn at different times. Tonight, we want to study a blend that has two sounds. It is "th." (Writes "th.") Sometimes this blend sounds "th" (breath sound), as in "think." Sometimes it sounds "th" (voice), as in "that." These blends are not very difficult for us to sound, but they are difficult for many foreign-born people. What we want to remember is that in making one of them—the one in "think"—we use only the breath. (Demonstrates.) In making the other—the one in "that" —we use the voice. (Demonstrates.) When I sound the "th" in "think," you hear only the hissing of my breath. (Demonstrates.) When I sound the "th" in "that," you hear the sound of my voice, don't you? (Demonstrates.) Will you sound the "th" in "think" with me?
TEACHER AND CLASS: "Th" (breath sound).
TEACHER: Will you sound the "th" in "that," with me?
TEACHER AND CLASS: "Th" (voice).
TEACHER: Suppose we think of a few words for each of the "th" blends. Let's take the breath blend first. Who will give me a word?
CLASS: (No answer.)
TEACHER: Suppose we open our books and look for words that have "th" in them. It doesn't matter whether the "th" is at the beginning, in the middle or at the end of the word. We can test them out and see whether they are made with breath only or with the voice. (Books are opened.) As soon as you find one, let us know.

FIRST PUPIL: I have found "this."

TEACHER: Listen while I sound it slowly. (Sounds "th-i-s.") Will you make those three sounds with me?

TEACHER AND CLASS: "Th-i-s."

TEACHER: Do you hear any voice in the first sound?

SEVERAL PUPILS: Yes, we do.

TEACHER: Good. Then let's write that over here as we are looking for the breath sounds now. (Writes "this.")

PUPIL: I have found "with."

TEACHER: Good. Listen while I sound it slowly. (Sounds "w-i-th.") Now, will you sound it with me?

TEACHER AND CLASS: "W-i-th."

PUPIL: That has voice in it, too.

TEACHER: Yes, it has. So I will write it under "this."

PUPIL: I have found "them."

TEACHER: Class, as soon as I sound "them" will you call out, "breath" or "voice"? (Sounds "th-e-m.")

SEVERAL PUPILS: Voice.

TEACHER: We seem to be finding only voice blends, don't we? (Writes "them" under "with.")

PUPIL: I have found "t-h-i-n-g." (Spells.)

TEACHER: That belongs to one of our word families, doesn't it? Who will tell us to which family it belongs?

SEVERAL PUPILS: It belongs to the "ing" family.

TEACHER: Good. I am so glad you found that word, Mr. Corn, because it is made up of just two parts and we know both of them. So we can soon know what the word is. First we have our blend "th." Let's try the breath "th" first as that is the one we especially want to find right now. (Sounds "th" with breath.) We know the rest of the word is "ing," don't we? So we have "th-ing." (Sounds.)

SEVERAL PUPILS: It is "thing," isn't it? And now we have one more breath blend for our list.

TEACHER: Excellent. (Writes "thing" under "think.")

PUPIL: I have found "t-h-a-n-k." (Spells.)

TEACHER: That word belongs to the "ank" family, so I shall sound it this way—"th-ank."

CLASS: Breath!

TEACHER: It surely is. (Writes "thank" under "thing.") Suppose we find one more. Oh, I have just thought of two and both of them are breath blends. They are "th-ick" and "th-in."

CLASS: Good! (Laughter.)

TEACHER: Since you like those two, suppose I give two for the voice blends—"they" and "those." (Writes.)

CLASS: Excellent! Now, won't you please make us a type sentence for each of the "th" blends? (Laughter.)

TEACHER: I shall be glad to make the two type sentences, if you will repeat them with me and if you will be sure to remember them until the next lesson.

CLASS: We will do our best.

TEACHER: One sentence is—"Think and thank through thick and thin."

SEVERAL PUPILS: That is for the breath blend.

TEACHER: Very good indeed. The other sentence is—"They put these with those over there."

CLASS: That is the sentence for the voice blend. Now, won't you please repeat those two sentences with us, so that we may remember them?

TEACHER AND CLASS: "Think and thank through thick and thin."

"They put these with those over there."

### Follow Up Work

Find two words that have "th" in them. Copy these words in your notebook.

## Lesson XX

TEACHER: In our last lesson, class, we studied a blend that had two sounds, didn't we? What was the difference in the two sounds?

CLASS: One was made with the breath and the other with the voice.

TEACHER: Good. Will you sound the breath blend and give its type sentence?

CLASS: "Th." "Think and thank through thick and thin."

TEACHER: Excellent! Will you sound the voice blend and give its type sentence?

CLASS: "They put these with those over there."

TEACHER: You did remember both of them, didn't you? Good for you! I have been thinking that you might like to decide which of the consonants are made with the voice and which with the breath only. I will make two columns and will write "Breath" over one and "Voice" over the other. Then, after we decide, I will write each consonant in the proper column. (Writes.) To make it simpler, I will make a list of the consonants for us to look at. (Writes b, c, d, f, g, h, j, k, l, m, n, p, q, r, s, t, v, w, x, y, z.) Will you copy this list right away and draw a line under the consonants that belong in the "Voice" column? (Pupils copy consonants in note books and underline those they believe to be "Voice" consonants.)

TEACHER: Mrs. Wallen, will you read us the letters that you think should go in the "Voice" column? And while she reads, class, will you watch your list and let us know when you do not agree with her? All right Mrs. Wallen, please give us the "Voice" consonants.

Mrs. Wallen: b, d.

Pupil: Shouldn't she have one of the c's for a "Voice" consonant?

Teacher: Suppose we sound them and see.

Teacher and Class: "c" (hard), "c" (soft).

Several Pupils: They are both "breath" letters.

Mrs. Wallen: g, j, l, m, n, p.

Pupil: I thought "p" was a "breath" letter.

Mrs. Wallen: It surely is. I don't know how I happened to put that down. I'll strike it out and go on with the others—q, r, s (one of them), v, w, x.

Pupil: Isn't "x" the one that is like "ks"? It seems to me it is a "breath" letter.

Mrs. Wallen: That's right, too. Now, that I've thought about it again, I'm sure you are right. My other two "voice" consonants are "y" and "z".

Teacher: Isn't that well done, class? She missed only two of the whole list. How many did as well as that? (Five hands are raised.)

Teacher: Excellent! Now, we are ready to fill in our "voice" column, aren't we? (Writes.)

### Voice Consonants

| | |
|---|---|
| b | q |
| d | r |
| g | s (one of them) |
| j | v |
| l | w |
| m | y |
| n | z |

And as those that are left must be the "breath" consonants, we can fill in that column, too, can't we? (Writes.)

### Breath Consonants

| | |
|---|---|
| c | p |
| f | s (one of them) |
| h | t |
| k | x |

What about the vowels, class, are they made with the voice or with the breath only? Suppose we sound first the long vowels and then the short ones and find out.

Teacher and Class: a, e, i, o, u (Long sounds).

a, e, i, o, u (Short sounds).

SEVERAL PUPILS: All of them are "voice" letters.

TEACHER: Good. Now, suppose we decide something else about the consonant sounds. Let's decide which are easy to make, which are less easy and which are difficult. Will you just put them in three columns in your notebooks, putting the easy ones in the first column, the less easy ones in the second and the difficult ones in the third column? (Pupils make the three columns.)

TEACHER: Now, I am going to put my columns on the board. Then we can all sound the letters and find out if those I have called easy are easy and if those that I think are difficult are difficult. (Writes.)

| Easy | Less Easy | Difficult |
|------|-----------|-----------|
| c, c | n | b |
| f | q | d |
| h | r | g |
| k | v | j |
| l | w | y |
| m | x | |
| p | | |
| s, s | | |
| t | | |
| z | | |

Suppose we try all of the sounds in my "Easy" column. (Pupils sound the ten easy letters, two-thirds of the class having no difficulty.)

TEACHER: Excellent. Don't you believe we can let that column stand as it is?

CLASS: That is all right. They are not hard.

TEACHER: Now, for those that are not quite so easy. (Pupils sound the six less easy letters, about half the class having difficulty with some, or all, of them.)

SEVERAL PUPILS: That column is all right, too.

TEACHER: Then let's try the difficult column. (Pupils try to make the five difficult sounds. About one-third of the pupils can sound them fairly well.)

PUPIL: Nobody can deny that those sounds are hard to make.

TEACHER: That is true. And yet quite a good many of us can make them and nearly all of us know them when we hear them, don't we? And aren't you a little bit surprised to find how few of them are really hard for you now?

PUPIL: I surely am surprised. If anybody had asked me, I should have said that I knew about half of them. And now I see that I know all but three or four of them. It has made me think of a plan for our closing exercises next week. Don't you believe if we made a list of the things we have learned in these twenty lessons and had one of the pupils read it at the closing exercises, everybody would be as surprised and interested as we are?

TEACHER: What a splendid idea, Mrs. Wilson. That will be really interesting to everybody. Suppose we write it all down right now, so whoever is to read it next week, can take it home tonight and practice reading it. Suppose we begin it this way (writes): "In our twenty lesson course in Phonics, this is what we have learned—" Then, we can think of the different things and write them below. What are some of the things?

FIRST PUPIL: We have learned the sounds of nearly all of the consonants and of all the long and short vowels.

SECOND PUPIL: We have learned some of the word families and some of the blends.

THIRD PUPIL: We have learned how to spell words better from knowing the sounds of the letters, blends, and word families. When I began, if you had asked me to spell "book," I should have been just as likely as not to have begun it with "h" or "y" instead of "b."

FOURTH PUPIL: We have learned how to puzzle out new words—to look for the parts we know and not try to swallow the word whole.

TEACHER: Class, you have done that wonderfully well. I am going to write down exactly what you have said. It will make a happy ending for our adventure in Phonics. (Writes.) In our twenty lesson course in Phonics, this is what we have learned:

1. The sounds of nearly all of the consonants.
2. The sounds of the long and the short vowels.
3. Some of the word families.
4. Some of the blends.
5. How to spell words better from knowing the sounds of the letters.
6. How to puzzle out new words.

.

www.ingramcontent.com/pod-product-compliance
Lightning Source LLC
Chambersburg PA
CBHW030650270326
41929CB00007B/299